CAREER SKILLS LIBRARY

Learning
the Ropes

THIRD EDITION

CAREER SKILLS LIBRARY

Communication Skills

Finding A Job

Leadership Skills

Learning the Ropes

Organization Skills

Problem Solving

Professional Ethics and Etiquette

Research and Information Management

Teamwork Skills

FERGUSON

CAREER SKILLS LIBRARY

Learning the Ropes

THIRD EDITION

Ferguson Publishing
An imprint of Infobase Publishing

Learning the Ropes, Third Edition

Copyright © 1998, 2004, 2009 by Infobase Publishing

Ferguson
An imprint of Infobase Publishing
132 West 31st Street
New York NY 10001

Library of Congress Cataloging-in-Publication Data

Learning the ropes / Facts On File. — 3rd ed.
    p. cm. — (Career skills library)
  Includes bibliographical references and index.
  ISBN-13: 978-0-8160-7775-5 (hardcover : alk. paper)
  ISBN-10: 0-8160-7775-4 (hardcover : alk. paper) 1. Vocational guidance.
2. Work. I. Ferguson Publishing.
  HF5381.N363 2009
  650.1—dc22
                          2009008629

Ferguson books are available at special discounts when purchased in bulk quantities for businesses, associations, institutions, or sales promotions. Please call our Special Sales Department in New York at (212) 967-8800 or (800) 322-8755.

You can find Ferguson on the World Wide Web at http://www.fergpubco.com

Text design by David Strelecky, adapted by Erik Lindstrom
Cover design by Takeshi Takahashi
First edition by Joe Mackall

Printed in the United States of America

MP ML 10 9 8 7 6 5 4 3 2 1

This book is printed on acid-free paper.

CONTENTS

Part III: Your Rights and Obligations as an Employee

Part IV: Troubleshooting

INTRODUCTION

Each year as you return to school, there are certain things you know you will face. You know you will have classes to attend and that you will have to get to them on time. You know you will have tests to study for and take and that your success on those tests will depend on plenty of preparation and focused performance. There will be teachers to listen to and respect and classmates who will be your partners and, at times, your competitors. Sure, you know that each year will bring plenty of new things to learn, but you have a grasp of the basics and are thus prepared to face those challenges.

Now that you're starting to think about entering the workplace, you'll be glad to know it works the same way. If you have a grasp of the basics, you have the tools and skills necessary to progress and succeed in your job.

Think about it like this: When you're facing your first day on the job, just like your first day of school, there are certain givens. You know you'll have a work schedule, perhaps Monday through Friday,

If you have a grasp of the basics, you have the tools and skills necessary to progress and succeed in your job.

Learning the ropes is part of any job, whether you are working at an after-school job or are fresh out of college starting a new career. (Frank Ordonez, Syracuse Newspapers/ The Image Works)

and that you'll have to get to work on time. There will be tasks to prepare for and complete, and your success on those tasks will depend on preparation and focused performance. You know you'll have a boss—maybe several—to listen to and respect and that your coworkers will be your partners and, at times, your competitors. There's still plenty to learn, but by gaining a firm grasp of the basics found in this book, you'll be ready to enter the challenging world of work.

FACTS AND FIGURES

- Number of people in the civilian labor force age 16 and older: 154,616,000

- Average unemployment rate among workers age 16 and older: 6.7 percent

- Approximately 79.6 percent of all young people age 16–19 are participating in the labor force.

Source: U.S. Bureau of Labor Statistics (November 2008)

The lessons in this book are not just for entry-level workers. Every person in every career—from your teacher to Will Smith to Donald Trump—utilizes the basic skills in this book. Perfecting these skills is the basis of how they succeed in their jobs, and it's the basis of how you'll succeed in yours.

Fortunately, you've already learned many lessons in your school career. These will prove invaluable in your work career.

This book is divided into four main parts.

- Part I describes the typical structure of a business, the concept of profit, and the types of management.

10 LESSONS FROM SCHOOL THAT ALSO WORK ON THE JOB

1. Be on time.

2. Be prepared.

3. Listen for instructions first.

4. Ask questions if you don't understand.

5. Don't let your personal life distract you from the tasks at hand.

6. Give 100 percent effort.

7. Respect your superiors.

8. Respect your colleagues.

9. Gain big rewards from extra credit.

10. Learn from your mistakes.

- Part II discusses some of the topics to prepare you for your first day of work and beyond, such as first-day jitters, dress codes, realistic job expectations, and dealing with your coworkers.

- Part III addresses some of your rights as an employee.

- Part IV provides tips on handling some potentially troublesome workplace scenarios, such as office conflicts, asking for a raise, and leaving a job.

PART I

Basic Business Structure

1

THIS IS YOUR MISSION

Every company has *business missions*, which are long-range goals the company wants to achieve in order to be a success. The following are some examples of common business missions:

- Produce top-quality merchandise
- Offer merchandise at affordable prices
- Gain customer loyalty and repeat business
- Gain a positive reputation in the market
- Make a profit (the bigger the better)

As you prepare for any new job, you must have a general grasp of your employer's business mission. For example, two coffee shop co-owners may have a mission to serve the best coffee at an affordable price. They want customers to consider their shop the best coffeehouse in town and to keep coming back. Most of all, the owners want to make a profit so that they can stay in business and make more money.

✔ TRUE OR FALSE?

Do You Know Your Mission?

1. I don't need to know my company's mission. I just need to show up on time, do my work, and I'll receive a paycheck.

Test yourself as you read through this chapter. The answer appears on page 9.

There is no truer and more abiding happiness than the knowledge that one is free to go on doing, day by day, the best work one can do, in the kind one likes best, and that this work is absorbed by a steady market and thus supports one's own life.

—Robin George Collingwood, English philosopher and historian

✍ EXERCISE

Imagine you're starting a lawn-care business. Answer these two questions.

- What are the missions of my company?
- What role will the people I employ play in fulfilling my company's missions?

So where do you fit into your company's business mission? As the person behind the counter, the one making and serving up the coffee and cinnamon rolls, *you* must take on the business's mission. Your friendly service, competence, and willingness to take care of the customer are main ingredients in your company's success. As an employee, your business's mission becomes your mission.

✔ TRUE OR FALSE: ANSWER

Do You Know Your Mission?

1. I don't need to know my company's mission. I just need to show up on time, do my work, and I'll receive a paycheck.

False. Knowing your company's mission—the goals it wants to achieve as a result of doing business—will help you do your job better.

IN SUMMARY . . .

- Business missions are a company's goals and objectives.
- To participate in any business venture, you must know your company's mission, and you must understand your place in that mission.

2

PROFITS

The ultimate goal of any business is to make a profit, or more income than what is needed to cover business expenses. Think about profits in terms of simple math. If the local sandwich-shop owner spends $700 a week to buy all the sandwich fixings, pay his employees, and pay for the rent on his shop, he won't stay in business long if he only takes in $400 a week in sales. His expenses would be greater than his income. In order to stay in business and be a success, the sandwich-shop owner would have to make more than $700 a week.

The company you work for also has to make more money than it spends in order to be successful. This is what everyone who works for the company is working together to do.

The following sections clear up some common questions and misconceptions about profits.

NONPROFIT ORGANIZATIONS

A *nonprofit organization* is not out to make money for itself above and beyond the cost of its operations.

✔ TRUE OR FALSE?

Do You Understand Profits?

1. Good employees help their companies generate profits by avoiding unnecessary expenditures and reducing waste.

Test yourself as you read through this chapter. The answer appears on page 14.

Think about it like this: You've heard the words "This is a nonprofit organization" on television, perhaps during an infomercial for a charity. That means all of the organization's profits—money left over after supplies are bought, office space is rented, and workers paid—go into a fund used for some purpose by a charity or social organization.

Your role in a nonprofit organization is no different from your role in a for-profit company. You still have to work hard to meet your obligations as an employee to ensure that the organization generates more money than it spends, enabling it to give to charity or fund social programs.

PROFIT AND REVENUE

Profit and revenue are different things. *Revenue* is all the money received from customers as payment for sales or services. Think of revenue as all the money in the cash register at the end of the day. Revenue pays for business expenses. The money that is left over is profit.

PROFIT AND YOUR PAYCHECK

You may be wondering if your paycheck will be affected if your company does not make a profit. The answer is no, at least not in the short run. The company considers employee paychecks as a fixed expense, just like your family might have mortgage or car payments as fixed expenses. Your pay is figured into the accounting so that even if the company doesn't make much above its expenses, you still get paid. This is not ideal, though. If the company where you work is continually paying worker salaries when it isn't making much money, you should probably start looking for another job. If this situation doesn't improve, the company probably will go out of business soon.

Work saves us from three great evils: boredom, vice, and need.

—Voltaire, French philosopher

As an employee, you play an important part in the earning of profits. It's your work as a good employee that keeps customers coming back, which in turn pays the company's bills. The customer's money goes into the cash register as revenue. Also, good employees

Good employees help generate profits by preventing waste and avoiding unnecessary expenses.

help generate profits by preventing waste and avoiding unnecessary expenses. Employees who increase revenue or find ways to decrease expenses contribute directly to their company's profits, which could lead to salary increases and fast promotions.

✔ TRUE OR FALSE: ANSWER

Do You Understand Profits?

1. Good employees help their companies generate profits by avoiding unnecessary expenses and reducing waste.

True. Do everything possible to help your company be successful and stay in business. Fewer in-house expenditures allow companies to spend more money developing new products, creating marketing campaigns, and, theoretically, paying higher salaries to their workers.

IN SUMMARY . . .

- Even nonprofit organizations must make money in order to pay their fixed expenses and to continue to operate.

- Revenue is all money taken in by a business before expenses are paid.

- Profit is the amount of money left over after all expenses have been paid.

- Generating profit is the end goal for not only business owners, but for their employees as well.

3

THE
MANAGEMENT

The structure of personnel in your workplace is likely to follow this model.

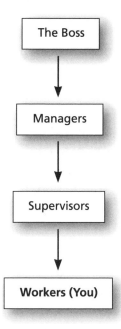

✔ TRUE OR FALSE?

Do You Understand Management Structure?

1. The boss is always right.

Test yourself as you read through this chapter. The answer appears on page 23.

The boss is at the top of the list, since he or she will have the most responsibility. It's your boss that keeps things running in the office, and the right to hire or fire you ultimately rests in his or her position. The boss must make sure that all the workers, including you, are doing their jobs and that all jobs are completed satisfactorily.

"It is my responsibility to make sure that my employees follow the parameters I have set up for a project," says Jason Smith, a manager at a graphic design firm. "These involve quality standards, due dates, and any special requests from the customer." Smith has a responsibility to complete the job on time so that his clients are satisfied with his company's work. He has to be able to depend on his employees to take their work seriously and to give it their best effort.

The entire structure of the business depends greatly on the boss keeping things running.

The entire structure of the business depends greatly on the boss keeping things running. In almost any company with more than a dozen employees, there are managers or supervisors who directly oversee day-to-day operations and to whom employees report. In even larger companies, there is often another layer of supervisors working under managers. Typically, supervisors instruct and monitor the workers in their daily tasks. As a new employee, your direct supervisor will often be someone who has just a few years more on-the-job experience than you.

THE CUSTOMER IS ALWAYS RIGHT

A basic principle common to nearly every successful business is "the customer is always right." That means if the customer says he didn't order the side of coleslaw even though you know he did, you must

It is important to remember that your customer—whether it is a person buying a cup of coffee or a client purchasing thousands of dollars worth of services or products—is always right. Keep the customer happy, and your boss will be happy, too. (C.W. McKeen, Syracuse Newspapers/The Image Works)

give him the side of fries he's now swearing he did order. Even when customers are in the wrong, good service dictates that the customer is always right.

Your boss probably knows about this principle. Chances are that he or she has been called over many times by a disgruntled customer. In such cases, your boss probably apologized graciously and calmed the customer with a bit of personal attention and a quick fix to the complaint. "The customer is always right" is also a vital part of your job as a worker. Keeping customers happy and coming back for more is the best guarantee of your own job security.

There is only one boss. The customer. And he can fire everybody in the company from the chairman on down, simply by spending his money somewhere else.

—Sam Walton, founder of Wal-Mart

IS THE BOSS ALWAYS RIGHT?

Not always. The boss is the authority figure in the workplace, so you do have to do what he or she asks of you when it comes to scheduling and job responsibilities. This doesn't, however, mean that the boss can make you work 90 hours a week, steal your lunch money, borrow your car at will, or ask you to do something illegal or unethical. There are limits to

Sam Walton, the founder of Wal-Mart Stores Inc., believed that the customer was the ultimate boss. (AP Photo)

your boss's power. Your boss is there to instruct you and to organize an efficient workplace.

GET ON YOUR BOSS'S GOOD SIDE

Your boss is one of the most important people in your career. If you get along well with your boss, your chances of being promoted or receiving a raise will greatly increase. If you don't get along with your boss, your career advancement may slow and you may even lose your job. Here are a few suggestions that will help you stay on good terms with your boss:

Know your boss's likes and dislikes. What are your boss's pet peeves? What is his or her preferred method of communication—telephone, email, or memo? Is your manager a morning or an afternoon person? Is your boss a hands-on or hands-off manager? You get the idea. By learning your manager's personality quirks, you can carefully modulate your behavior and performance to match his or her needs.

Solve your boss's problems. Most likely, your boss has a boss. Try to think of what you can do to make your manager's life easier and allow him or her to shine with upper management.

Avoid making unreasonable requests. Don't pester your boss with constant requests for higher pay, promotions, or extra days off.

Hone your reputation. Develop a good reputation in the office—it will reflect positively on your manager. You can develop a good reputation by being a hard worker, not complaining about your company or boss to coworkers, always meeting deadlines, being nice to others, giving the extra effort, and being organized.

Avoid surprises. No boss likes to find out at the last minute that you're running late on a project. Keep your manager apprised of your progress on work assignments, and never wait till the last minute to ask for extra time, resources, etc.

Never embarrass your boss. Don't complain about your manager to your coworkers; whether the criticism is warranted or not, it drags down his or her standing in the office. Always share bad news or project developments with your boss so that he or she is not blindsided when asked about these issues by peers, superiors, or the press.

FINDING COMMON GROUND

You have a lot more in common with your boss than you think. You're both working for the ultimate success of the business. Your boss was once a worker as you are now. He or she learned the basics of the workplace, mastered them, and used them to advance from worker, to manager, to supervisor, to boss. The next section examines the basics of fitting into your job so that you may learn and excel—and perhaps someday be the boss yourself.

✔ TRUE OR FALSE: ANSWER

Do You Understand Management Structure?

1. The boss is always right.

False. You should do whatever he or she asks in regard to scheduling and job responsibilities, but you never should feel compelled to do anything illegal or unethical.

IN SUMMARY . . .

- Your supervisors, managers, and bosses are all working toward the same goal as you: to promote business and keep it running smoothly.

- Though often difficult, doing everything possible to make sure the customer or client is satisfied is good for business.

- Your boss is the authority figure. In terms of job responsibilities, you should do everything he or she asks. But you should never do anything that is illegal or unethical.

- By making your boss's life easier, you make your own easier—and improve your chances of keeping your job and even getting a raise or a promotion.

PART II
Fitting in at Work

4

YOUR FIRST DAY

The beginning is the most important part of the work.

—Plato, Greek philosopher

Everyone is a little nervous on his or her first day of work. Palms sweat, mouths get dry, and words are not strung together eloquently. First-day jitters are a uniting factor for every person in the workplace: Everyone's had that shaky, unsure first day—and all have survived it.

"When I walked through the doors on my first day of work," recalls Steve Blahitka of his summer job at NFL Films, "my mind was filled with all sorts of questions and worries. Would I fit in? Would the people here like me? How long would it take me to figure out what I'm supposed to be doing? And," he laughs, "how long before I can ask for a day off?"

Blahitka's questions are very common among new workers. You walk into an unfamiliar functioning environment, and without much formal instruction

✔ TRUE OR FALSE?

Are You Ready for Your First Day?

1. Being nervous on the first day of work is natural.

2. It's important to make a good impression on your first day at work.

3. If I'm new to the office, I should probably wait a few weeks until I introduce myself to my coworkers.

Test yourself as you read through this chapter. The answers appear on pages 39–41.

you're supposed to join in and keep the "machine" working smoothly.

The following are some common first-day fears you might experience:

- No one will like me.
- I'll make a mistake.
- I won't catch on.
- My boss won't like me.
- I won't be able to do the job.
- I'll get lost.
- I'll ask stupid questions.
- I won't remember anyone's name.
- I'll be embarrassed.

✍ EXERCISE

Look at the preceding list of common first-day fears. Circle one that might most apply to your own feelings on your first day. What could you do to allay this fear?

If you picked "no one will like me" from the list, consider this question: When was the last time you entered a situation in which literally no one liked you? How likely is it that the receptionists, the office workers, the boss, the cleaning team, and even the photocopier repair technician will run screaming from the room when you walk in? How likely is it that the people you work with will decide to give you the cold shoulder? How likely is it that you will be so hated in your new workplace that you'll be forced to work alone, eat lunch alone, or have your desk moved into the basement where no one has to deal with you? These examples are a bit extreme, but they illustrate the irrationality of your fears.

If one of your worst fears is "I'll make a mistake," consider this: Expect to make mistakes, and have no fear of making them. Why? We all learn from mistakes, and as the new person in the office, it's almost expected that you'll make them.

Many of your first-day fears are completely natural and completely expected. Also, they are a vital part of learning the ropes at your new workplace. As for the fear of getting fired on your first day, you would

We all learn from mistakes, and as the new person in the office, it's almost expected that you'll make them.

have to work pretty hard to mess up that horribly. Plus, you're likely to get a break as "the new kid on the block." Your boss and coworkers won't expect you to perform miracles during your first week on the job.

A life spent in making mistakes is not only more honorable but more useful than a life spent doing nothing.

—**George Bernard Shaw,**
Irish playwright

TEN FIRST-DAY GOALS

There are goals to accomplish before you even get to work. You need to wake up early to ensure that you get to work on time—or even ahead of schedule. You also need to dress appropriately for your first day on the job (see Chapter 5 for more information on dressing for success).

Once you get to work, your first and most obvious step is to find out where you're supposed to be and what you're supposed to be doing. Usually, your boss or a supervisor will greet you and lead you into the workplace, where you'll be introduced around, given a tour, and acquainted with the basics of your job. Perhaps you'll be led to your desk or workstation, given tax forms to fill out, a box of pens, and a key to the bathroom. Whatever your first few hours are

Your first day on the job will involve many challenges—including learning how to use office equipment such as a photocopier. (John Birdsall, The Image Works)

like, there are fundamental goals you should cover on your first day so you'll be ready to work the following day.

I am an experienced registered nurse, and I enjoy broadening my scope of practice by trying new areas of nursing. I have worked in orthopedic, hematology/oncology, and interventional radiology nursing, and now in the emergency department in a hospital setting. I offer the following advice to new nurses who start out in our department: observe; don't be afraid to ask questions; understand the culture of the workplace and what is expected of you in your new role; be friendly and accommodating to your coworkers, but try to set yourself apart by not participating in idle gossip; read up on new developments in the field, and take continuing education classes pertinent to your field. By doing all these things you will become an invaluable member of any team. You will be noticed, and your boss and peers will respect your example.

—Vanessa Woroszylo, registered nurse

10 GOALS FOR YOUR FIRST DAY ON THE JOB

1. Dress for success.

2. Get to work early.

3. Meet your boss.

4. Meet your coworkers.

5. Meet other office workers.

6. Find your desk.

7. Find your boss's office.

8. Find necessary areas such as the copy room, break room, restroom, and lunchroom.

9. Establish your position in a friendly manner.

10. Establish your presence in a friendly manner.

FIRST IMPRESSIONS

You've heard the expression "first impressions count." The minute you walk in the door, what the boss and the office workers see of you is going to color their first impressions of you. Do you look professional? Do you look serious about working at this job? Do you take care to present yourself in the best possible manner? If the answers to these questions are yes, you've qualified yourself for respect and a welcome to the office.

Is it fair that people can make snap preliminary judgments about your character and professionalism based solely on how your hair is styled, how you've chosen to dress, how you walk, or the tone of your voice? Perhaps not, but it's a fact of the workplace. In the business world, a professional image is going to establish you as a serious worker.

DID YOU KNOW?

Seventy percent of employers surveyed by The Conference Board in 2006 rated high school graduates as deficient in professionalism/work ethic. Nearly 20 percent of college graduates were considered deficient in these areas.

Source: *Are They Really Ready to Work?*

The first impression you make is likely to be a lasting one, so keep in mind that you're sending clear messages to everyone around you when you walk through the door. With each hand you shake and

✍ EXERCISE

Read the following two examples:

Worker #1 walks into the office. He's wearing wrinkled pants and sneakers, and his hair hasn't been combed. He keeps his hands in his pockets when he meets the boss, and he doesn't crack a smile or make eye contact with anyone when he's introduced around the office. He shuffles his feet, slouches, doesn't ask any questions, and looks at the clock three times before 11:00 A.M.

Worker #2 walks into the office. He's dressed in a pair of dress slacks, a white shirt, and a tie. He's wearing a pair of dress shoes. He's clean-cut and freshly shaven. He smiles at the receptionist and shakes hands with the boss who comes to greet him. He nods hello at office workers and listens intently as everything is explained to him. He asks questions in a friendly manner and seems pleased to work there.

- Who do you think makes the best first impression?
- Whom do you resemble?
- What can you do to make the best first impression?

each person you meet, you're saying whether or not you're to be taken seriously, respected, and welcomed as a member of the team.

A SUCCESSFUL FIRST DAY

Sally walks with confidence through the doors of the office building. She's greeted by her smiling supervisor, given the grand tour, and introduced to her coworkers. Once Sally has established her space in the office, gotten her bearings, filled out paperwork, and asked any questions she might have, she's ready to learn about her job.

She follows the cues of her coworkers, such as when to leave for lunch, how early to arrive at staff meetings, and how to send mail. When she has a

In the business world, a professional image is going to establish you as a serious worker.

SURF THE WEB: HOW TO ACT AND PERFORM AT WORK

About.com: Workplace Survival and Success
http://careerplanning.about.com/
od/workplacesurvival/Workplace_
Survival_and_Success.htm

First Day on the Job
http://www.laworks.net/Youth_Portal/
YP_Forms/YP_FirstDay.pdf

GradView
http://www.gradview.com/careers/
etiquette.html

TO BE SUCCESSFUL ON YOUR FIRST DAY ON THE JOB, YOU SHOULD:

• Be friendly

• Be a good listener

• Have confidence

• Be professional

• Have strong communication skills

• Have a good memory (names, tasks, etc.)

• Be positive

• Treat others with respect

question about using her phone or where to sign a document, she asks her nearest coworker for assistance and thanks her for the help.

During Sally's break, she walks around the office, learning the locations of storage rooms, the mailroom, and senior staffers' offices.

At lunch she eats in the lunchroom with the other workers, introducing herself to those she might not have met, and finding some common ground with them all. After lunch, she continues with her tasks until it's time to leave. She departs for home confident that she has a solid preliminary grasp of the job.

✍ EXERCISE

What is an example of a more subtle action that could give your boss, teacher, coworkers, or classmates the wrong impression of you? Have you ever made the mistake of acting this way? How did you "right" the wrong impression?

SURF THE WEB: HELP WITH OFFICE EQUIPMENT

Expert Village: Learn Basic Computer Skills
http://www.expertvillage.com/video-series/528_computer-filing-system-windows.htm

How Stuff Works: How Fax Machines Work
http://communication.howstuffworks.com/fax-machine4.htm

How Stuff Works: How Virtual Offices Work
http://communication.howstuffworks.com/virtual-office.htm

How to Use a Scanner
http://www.aarp.org/learntech/computers/howto/Articles/a2002-07-16-scan.html

HOW TO AVOID FIRST-DAY JITTERS: DON'T GET HIRED!

If you never get hired to begin with, you'll never have to worry about your first day at work. While this isn't a book about how to conduct yourself during a job interview, many of the principles of interviewing for a job apply just as much to your first day on the job. In both cases, first impressions count!

While the examples of inappropriate interview behavior in "Unfortunate Interviews" are a bit

UNFORTUNATE INTERVIEWS

OfficeTeam, a leading staffing service, asked 150 senior executives at the 1,000 largest U.S. companies and 100 senior executives in Canada to recall "the most embarrassing job interview moments they had heard of or witnessed." Here are a few of their responses:

- "The candidate sent his sister to interview in his place."

- "The person was dancing during the interview. He kept saying things like, 'I love life!' and 'Oh yeah!'"

- "A job applicant came in for an interview with a cockatoo on his shoulder."

- "The candidate stopped the interview and asked me if I had a cigarette."

extreme, think about how more subtle inappropriate behavior on your first day might indicate disinterest in the job, disrespect for the boss, an eccentric streak, a propensity for lying, or a lack of intelligence.

✔ TRUE OR FALSE: ANSWERS

Are You Ready for Your First Day?

1. Being nervous on the first day of work is natural.

- "The candidate got his companies confused and repeatedly mentioned the strengths of a competing firm, thinking that's who he was interviewing with."

- "A guy called me by the wrong name during the entire interview."

- "We're a retail company, and when we asked the candidate why she wanted to work for us, she said she didn't want to work in retail anymore."

- "An interviewee put his bubble gum in his hand, forgot about it, and then shook my hand."

- "Someone showed up for an interview in pajamas and his hair not combed, like he had just rolled out of bed."

- "A candidate fell asleep during the interview."

True. Almost everyone is nervous on the first day of a new job. There are new people to meet, complicated tasks and skills to learn, and the gnawing fear that you may not fit in. Think about it this way: everyone has been in your shoes at one point or another. Your coworkers understand that you will be a little nervous or might make a few mistakes early on, and hopefully will try to do everything possible to help you get acclimated to your new job.

2. It's important to make a good impression on your first day at work.

True. First impressions mean a lot, so you want to make sure that you come across as friendly and professional. Remember to offer a firm handshake and make good eye contact when being introduced to your coworkers, dress appropriately, and listen closely to your boss's instructions regarding office procedures and your new duties.

3. If I'm new to the office, I should probably wait a few weeks until I introduce myself to my coworkers.

False. You need to introduce yourself, or at least say hello, to as many people as possible during your first day (or first week, if you work for a large company). You want to make a good impression, and if you wait weeks to introduce yourself, your coworkers may think you're standoffish or just plain weird.

IN SUMMARY . . .

- Being nervous on your first day of work is unavoidable, but also natural.

- Before beginning your first day, you should make a list of goals to accomplish to get started on the right foot.

- First impressions do count, even after the interview and job offer. Be sure to make a good impression on not only your boss, but your coworkers as well.

5

DRESS FOR SUCCESS

All businesses have some sort of dress code, since all businesses want their workers to maintain an appearance of professionalism. They want you to be clean-cut. They want you to look your best.

Picture a busy office: Phones are ringing, fax machines are printing important messages, and copy machines whirring and humming. Workers are dashing from one end of the office to the other, delivering important packets and carrying files. Picture all of these people in faded jeans, T-shirts, and ratty old sneakers. You get a certain sense of the place, don't you? You might assume this is the office of a high school newspaper.

Now picture this same office scene with the workers in suits, dress shirts, dresses, and shined shoes. Do you have a different image of the office now? Suddenly the scene takes on a sense of professionalism. The workers may even look older to you.

✔ TRUE OR FALSE?

Do You Know How to Dress for Success?

1. I can wear whatever I want to work.

2. On casual Fridays, I can wear shorts, a T-shirt, and flip flops.

3. Your coworkers and manager can provide you with visual cues on how to dress in the office.

Test yourself as you read through this chapter. The answers appear on pages 50–51.

Some bosses want you to look your best in order to give a message to the customers: We're a classy business, we're professionals, we're trustworthy, and you know you're in the right place when you deal with our employees.

LEARNING THE DRESS CODE

The best way to figure out what you should be wearing to the office is to look around. When you walk through the office during a job interview, or as you take the grand tour of the office on your first day, note how the employees in that office dress. If everyone is in suits and ties or nice pants and dress shirts, consider that attire to be the dress code.

You can also contact your new supervisor or human resources prior to your first day and ask about the

SAMPLE OFFICE DRESS CODE

All employees will maintain a professional appearance as outlined by the dress codes that follow:

- Men will wear business pants with or without a jacket, a button-down business shirt, and a tie.

- Women will wear dresses with stockings, business suits, or dress-pant sets.

- No sneakers, jeans, T-shirts, or shorts are to be worn.

company dress code. Most businesses outline this policy in a company handbook or memo.

UNIFORMS

If you have a job that requires a uniform, your bosses have told you exactly what to wear. Most companies will provide you with your uniform or reimburse you for this purchase. Your responsibility then is to maintain this uniform with the same kind of professionalism expected in any other office. You

SURF THE WEB: DRESSING FOR WORK

About.com: Business Casual Dress Code
http://humanresources.about.com/od/
glossaryd/g/dress_code.htm

About.com: How to Dress for Work and Interviews
http://careerplanning.about.com/cs/
dressingforwork/a/dress_success.htm

AskMen.com: Business Casual Outfits
http://www.askmen.com/fashion/trends/21_
fashion_men.html

Business Casual Attire
http://www.career.vt.edu/JOBSEARC/BusCasual.htm

How to Dress Business Casual—Men
http://www.ehow.com/how_41_dress-business-
casual.html

How to Dress Business Casual—Women
http://www.ehow.com/how_49_dress-business-
casual.html

wikiHow: How to Dress For Work
http://www.wikihow.com/Dress-for-Work

Yahoo! HotJobs: The Rules of Workplace Style
http://hotjobs.yahoo.com/career-articles-the_
rules_of_workplace_style-535

SURVEY SAYS: BETTER-DRESSED WORKERS CONSIDERED MORE PROFESSIONAL

Eighty-one percent of employees surveyed by OfficeTeam, a leading staffing service, believe that the manner in which a person dresses affects his or her professional image. "People tend to form immediate impressions of each other," says Diane Domeyer, executive director of OfficeTeam. "Dressing professionally provides instant credibility and signals to clients, customers, and colleagues that they're working with someone who takes the position seriously." Domeyer says the economic downturn has prompted workers to dress less casually in order to present a more professional image and reduce their chances of being laid off.

should keep your uniform clean, ironed, and free from stains and holes.

CASUAL FRIDAY

Many companies have adopted what is known as casual or dress-down Fridays. On the last day of the business week, workers are allowed to wear more casual office wear, rather than business suits and

If you are required to wear a uniform at work, be sure to keep it clean, ironed, and free of rips and stains. (Jack Kurtz, The Image Works)

dresses. This makes for a more relaxed, though still professional, atmosphere. Rules for casual Friday vary from office to office, so find out what is considered appropriate for your workplace or if your company even has such a policy.

You may be thinking, "Why is it so important to dress correctly? I can do my job just as well in jeans as I can in a suit and tie." Some bosses agree with this common complaint, and they allow their workers to

OFFICE WARDROBE DOS AND DON'TS

DO

- Adhere to office dress codes.
- Look to coworkers for wardrobe ideas.
- Maintain a professional image.
- Keep your clothes clean and pressed.
- Replace old, worn, inappropriate, or out-of-style clothes.
- Dress more professionally (jacket or suit) if you are unsure of what to wear in a particular work situation.

DON'T

- Defy office dress codes just to be different.
- Try to dress "sexy."
- Wear office clothes that don't fit you well.
- Wear dirty, wrinkled, or stained office clothes.
- Abuse the privilege of wearing more relaxed clothing on casual Friday.

report for duty in any outfit they please. Other bosses would fire you on the spot if you dared to show up in khaki pants and a T-shirt. The bottom line is that it's the office codes of conduct that rule. It's your job to know and abide by those codes whether they are formal or implied rules.

☞ FACT

If your job requires that you wear special clothes or uniforms on the job and the clothing is not suitable for everyday wear, you may be able to deduct the cost of these clothes from the amount owed on your income taxes. Examples of such workers include bus drivers, mail carriers, police officers, firefighters, nurses, and airline pilots.

✔ TRUE OR FALSE?

Do You Know How to Dress for Success?

1. I can wear whatever I want to work.

False. You can dress however you want when you go out with your friends, but not at work. Most companies have clear policies on workplace dress. If you follow these rules, you'll fit in faster and be considered a team player.

2. On casual Fridays, I can wear shorts, a T-shirt, and flip flops.

False. Perhaps if you work as a lifeguard you could do this, but not at most companies. On casual Fridays, rules for workplace attire are relaxed, but not completely eliminated.

3. Your coworkers and manager can provide you with visual cues on how to dress in the office.

True. Follow the lead of your coworkers or boss if you're unsure of what to wear at a trade show, conference, or holiday party.

IN SUMMARY . . .

- Look at your bosses and coworkers for clues as to how to dress in your work environment.

- Even though you probably will be able to work just as well in jeans and tennis shoes, wearing more formal business clothes exudes a more professional image to clients and customers.

- Uniforms, if required for your job, should be worn with the same amount of care as a business suit. In other words, uniforms should be clean and pressed.

- Though many businesses have adopted casual business dress codes, especially on Fridays, this should not be abused. Dress no more casually than your managers and other coworkers.

6

REALISTIC EXPECTATIONS

What do you expect from a good job? A hefty paycheck? A challenging workload? A full schedule? Overtime? These are some of the more obvious things you might expect from life in the workplace. What you may not think of at first are the things that make your job a nice place to be.

FAIRNESS

You should be treated fairly. You should be given an appropriate amount of work for your position, not every responsibility in the place. You should be given credit for your ideas and be rewarded with an honest day's pay for an honest day's work. In other words, you should be paid for eight hours if you've worked eight hours. (Your end of the bargain, though, is to work those eight hours.)

✔ TRUE OR FALSE?

What Do You Expect from Your Job?

1. I can take breaks whenever I want.

2. It's important to take any legitimate workplace issues to your boss.

3. It's okay to arrive a few minutes late to work every once in awhile.

Test yourself as you read through this chapter. The answers appear on pages 60–61.

DECENT TREATMENT

You should be spoken to with decency, not treated like a servant. Your coworkers should remember that even though you're the new guy on the block, you're still a person.

RESPECT FROM OTHERS

Your coworkers and bosses should treat you with basic human respect. This means calling you by your name as you would call them by theirs. It also means respecting your needs and understanding if you need clarification on an assignment.

Likewise, you should adopt the same attitude of respect for your coworkers.

KEY TRAITS OF MILLENIALS

Who is a Millenial? You are, if you were born between 1980 and 2000. Millenials, sometimes known as Gen Yers, often get a bad rap from the media and hiring managers. Studies occasionally support this negative view. For example, a study by NAS Recruitment Communications found that Millenials often prefer self-expression over self-control, are impatient and expect instant gratification, and don't take office dress codes seriously. While these attitudes and behaviors may be true for some Millenials, they're definitely not the case for all. Millenials bring many unique talents and interests to the workplace. For example, studies show that Millenials:

- Are proficient with technology

- Understand the global economy and have often worked or studied abroad

- Are flexible and able to successfully multitask

- Enjoy learning and improving their skills

- Like to volunteer

- Are able to work well with others, including as part of a team

Do these skills describe you? If so, you're well on your way to becoming a productive member of the workforce. If not, work hard to develop the positive traits that are attributed to Millenials.

Sources: CareerVision; *Christian Science Monitor;*
Generation Y: The Millenials, Ready or Not, Here They Come

✍ EXERCISE

Write down your top 10 expectations for a good job.

UNREALISTIC EXPECTATIONS

There is such a thing as having unrealistic expectations, of course. If one of your expectations is taking breaks whenever you want, you have an unrealistic expectation of the workplace. Your boss is likely to be fair, perhaps giving you a break once or twice during your shift, but you shouldn't expect to be able to drop everything and wander outside for some fresh air whenever you feel like it.

Another unrealistic expectation is to want complete control over how you do things. Maybe you believe your way of writing a memo is better than the manager's method, but it's not up to you to override the decisions made by management. Remember your place in the personnel structure. For now, while you're a worker and not the boss, you'll have to follow company standards.

It's not up to you to override the decisions made by management.

The following are other unrealistic expectations you might have:

- I should get to boss around new workers.

- They should pay me for overtime. (Some companies don't.)

- I should get my birthday off.

- I should be able to arrange my work schedule around my social schedule.

- I don't want to be watched by my supervisor all the time.

SAFEGUARDING REALISTIC EXPECTATIONS

What if your realistic expectations are not being met? What if your boss talks to you like you're a child? What if hours keep disappearing from your timesheet, and your boss just shrugs and won't change your paycheck? What if you aren't treated fairly? In these cases, you have several options of action.

1. *Voice your concerns to the person who is disrespecting you.* Example: "Mary, it's not fair that you drop all your extra busywork on my desk just because I'm the new worker. I'd be glad to help you if I wasn't so swamped with work."

   "I'm sorry," Mary says, picking up the pile of papers she's just dropped on your desk. "It won't happen again."

2. *Explain your concerns to your boss.* Example: "Mr. Johnson, I'm unhappy with the way some of the workers keep dumping their busywork on me."

"Really?" Mr. Johnson says. "What do you mean?"

"The other day, for instance, one of the data-entry processors came by my desk and told me to photocopy a pile of papers for her. That's not in my job description, so I don't think I should let my responsibilities go just to do her busywork. I've brought that up to her and a few of the others."

"You're absolutely right," Mr. Johnson nods. "In the future, just tell any workers who attempt to get you to do their work that I have asked you to finish whatever project you're working on. And feel free to come to me if the problem persists."

3. *If the problems don't stop after you've tried to address them, find a different job.* Example: "Mr. Johnson, I've come to give you my two-week notice."

"You have?" says Mr. Johnson. "I'm sorry to hear that. May I ask why you're leaving us?"

"I feel like my expectations have not been met, in that I didn't receive the treatment I believe I deserve."

"Well, we're sorry to see you go," says Mr. Johnson.

If a job is truly not for you or if the workplace is not an acceptable environment, you should look for a better job. After giving a job your best shot, you're not a "quitter" if you walk away from a legitimately bad situation to find a better job.

☞ FACT

Giving your *two-week notice* means you'll be leaving the job in two weeks, and you'll remain on the job in the meantime while the company finds someone to replace you. It's a common courtesy.

YOUR BOSS'S EXPECTATIONS OF YOU

Just as you have every right to some realistic expectations of your job and workplace, your employer has the right to expect certain things from you. The following are some of your boss's realistic expectations that you should try your very best to meet:

- You will be a hard worker.
- You will be an honest worker.
- You will be competent in your job.
- You will work well with others.
- You will respect the boss.
- You will respect your supervisors.
- You will be dependable.
- You will follow all rules and policies.
- You will be punctual.

- You will keep the best interests of the company in mind.

✔ TRUE OR FALSE: ANSWERS

What Do You Expect from Your Job?

1. I can take breaks whenever I want.

False. You should always ask your supervisor for permission to take a break. If you decide to take a coffee break on a whim, you might be gone when your boss needs you to work on a pressing task.

2. It's important to take any legitimate workplace issues to your boss.

True. Your manager's job is to tell you what to do, but also to help you navigate the challenges of the workplace. If a personality conflict with a coworker, faulty equipment, or another issue keeps you from effectively doing your job, you need to alert your manager.

3. It's okay to arrive a few minutes late to work every once in awhile.

False. Always get to work on time or even ahead of time. You may think that arriving a few minutes late is no big deal, but imagine if everyone at your company had the same attitude. All those lost minutes over the course of a year add up. Think of all the projects that would never get started, deadlines that would never be met, phone calls and emails never returned.

IN SUMMARY . . .

- Both you and your boss should have realistic expectations of your job and workplace.

- You are entitled to be treated fairly, decently, and with respect.

- Your boss is entitled to your hard work, punctuality, and honesty.

- If you feel your rights as a worker are being violated you should (in the following order) confront the offending coworker, seek counsel from your boss, or look for another job.

7

THE DAILY GRIND

Now that you have a general picture of what's expected of you in a business structure, it's time for you to learn about functioning in the "daily grind," or the average workday.

The company you work for will have certain ground rules, which if broken could lead to disciplinary action or even termination of your employment. Thus it's a good idea to become familiar with these rules as soon as you can.

COMMON COMPANY RULES

Some companies give their new employees a handbook containing a list of company rules and regulations. Other companies expect you to use your common sense to lead your actions in the workplace. Whatever your company's approach, you can expect to see on any company-rules list, written or understood, the types of regulations listed here. Note that rules vary from company to company.

✔ TRUE OR FALSE?

Can You Handle the Daily Grind?

1. A little workplace gossip never hurt anyone.

2. I should ask the company president for help if my computer stops working.

3. There is no such thing as a stupid question.

Test yourself as you read through this chapter. The answers appear on page 72.

- No personal phone calls or texting.
- No personal visits during office hours.
- Requests for days off are to be submitted to the manager with 48 hours' notice.
- Employees may take 30 minutes for lunch and two 15-minute breaks during their day.
- No personal use of office equipment.
- Employees are to abide by office dress codes, including on casual Fridays.
- Workers are expected to be on time. Three late arrivals will result in disciplinary action.

If the last rule seems a bit extreme, you should know that punctuality is a very serious issue in the business world. Tardiness is not tolerated in school; if you're frequently tardy, you'll end up in detention or even suspended. It is even less tolerated in the workplace. Your boss is going to understand that unavoidable delays, like train delays or heavy traffic, sometimes happen. If you're a good worker and these occurrences are exceptions, your boss will give you the benefit of the doubt. However, if you are consistently late, you send a message to your boss that you're undependable, lazy, or just don't try to get to work on time. Your boss will expect you to leave home earlier if there is heavy traffic during your travel time. Most managers can spot a phony excuse a mile away.

Our management expects reliability in their subordinates in the form of showing up to work each day on time and being ready to perform our facility management roles in a focused and efficient manner. If we are not reliable, the company will become less profitable.

—Maria Gliane, senior chemical engineer, Abbott Laboratories

Showing up on time tells your boss that you're dependable, responsible, and organized. If you value your job, you should value the rules set for it.

ACCEPTABLE REASONS FOR BEING LATE

- Traffic incidents (accidents or road closures)

- Weather incidents (snow, icy roads, and heavy rainstorms)

- Car trouble

UNACCEPTABLE REASONS FOR BEING LATE

- Sleeping in (Solution: Always get a good night of sleep, save the late-nights out for weekends)

- Picking up breakfast/coffee (Solution: Have coffee and basic breakfast foods at the office in case you run late)

- Forgetting something (Solution: Make a list, place all work-related items in one place)

- Forgetting you had to work (Solution: Create a schedule you can post on a bulletin board or your refrigerator at home)

- Not able to get a ride (Solution: Buy a car or lease one in an emergency)

- Running out of gas (Solution: Always refill your tank when the fuel indicator reads half full)

If you are always running late for work, your manager may think that you do not take your job seriously. (Cameron/Corbis)

CHAIN OF COMMAND

One element you're sure to see on any list of company regulations is a chain of command. This is simply a chart of your bosses, listing the order in which you are to address issues with them. For instance, if you need to report a broken phone at your workstation, you will look at your chain of command to figure out whom to contact. You won't logically call the regional president of the company. You will probably tell your immediate supervisor. Here is a sample chain of command.

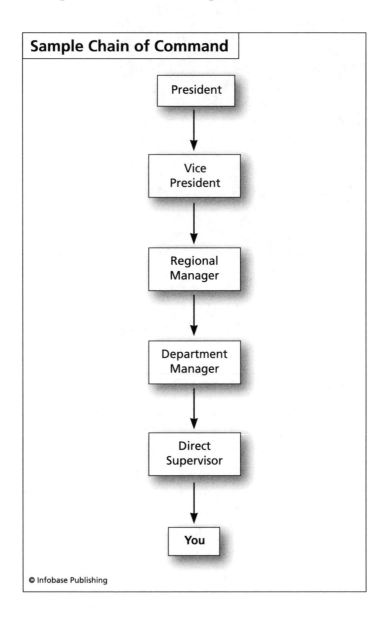

Sample Chain of Command

President

Vice President

Regional Manager

Department Manager

Direct Supervisor

You

It's important that you follow the chain of command when making a request or complaint. You don't want to go over your supervisor's head, ever. That will not only make you look bad, it'll make your supervisor look bad in the eyes of his bosses when he doesn't know anything about the information or the complaint.

—Captain Ronald Naylor, security supervisor

YOUR DAILY SCHEDULE

Your workday is likely to be governed by your daily schedule. Depending on your job and on your position in that job, your time line may be laid out as follows:

9:00–10:00 A.M.: Return phone calls

10:00–10:30 A.M.: Open and sort mail

10:30–10:45 A.M.: Coffee break

10:45 A.M.–12:30 P.M.: Work on accounts

12:30–1:30 P.M.: Lunch

1:30–3:30 P.M.: Work on accounts

3:30–3:45 P.M.: Coffee break

3:45–5:00 P.M.: Daily projects (outgoing mail, meetings, preparing reports)

Your boss establishes your schedule in order to give structure to your day and to keep you on track with the work you're supposed to do. It is your responsibility to adhere to this schedule and to complete all your tasks within it.

ASKING QUESTIONS

You've probably heard a thousand times from your teachers and coaches that "there's no such thing as a stupid question." The only stupid move you can make is *not* asking a question of your supervisor when you're not sure of something. Any boss would rather have you ask for clarification than proceed in an unsure way, possibly making a huge mistake that could cost the company time, money, or an entire account. Don't take chances; ask questions.

He who asks a question is a fool for five minutes; he who does not ask a question remains a fool forever.

—Chinese proverb

OFFICE POLITICS

In any office, there's a lot more going on than just the office work.

In any office, there's a lot more going on than just the office work. Your coworkers may be jockeying for position and favor in the eyes of the boss. Some coworkers may even organize into cliques that gossip about other coworkers. You may be tempted to participate in such gossip, take sides in arguments, and participate in covert hunts for information. You may think this sort of interaction makes you part

SURF THE WEB:
SURVIVING OFFICE POLITICS

About.com: Office Politics
  http://careerplanning.about.com/od/
  workplacesurvival/a/politics.htm

Ask Sue: Workplace Cliques
  http://www.careerknowhow.com/ask_sue/clique.
  htm

Monster.com: Winning at Office Politics: Master the
Game By Making Connections
  http://career-advice.monster.com/office-politics/
  diversity-inclusion/multicultural-workers/
  Winning-at-Office-Politics/home.aspx

Office-Politics
  http://www.officepolitics.com

of a group, but it's a dangerous game to play in the workplace. It is not unusual for management to take disciplinary action against employees who spread rumors or encourage office tension. If the damage inflicted by the rumors is serious enough, employees could lose their jobs.

To be safe, stay clear of all office politics. Don't take sides. Don't listen to or spread rumors. Just stick to your work—it's why you're there.

✔ TRUE OR FALSE: ANSWERS

Can You Handle the Daily Grind?

1. A little workplace gossip never hurt anyone.

False. Gossip creates cliques and negativity in the workplace and should be avoided.

2. I should ask the company president for help if my computer stops working.

False. Your company's president has neither the time nor most likely the skills to fix your malfunctioning CD drive or other computer problems. It's important to follow the chain of command in the workplace. If you have a problem (computer, incorrect pay stub, etc.), take it to your direct supervisor. He or she will be able to help you solve the problem or direct you to the appropriate person or department who can.

3. There is no such thing as a stupid question.

True. Your boss would much rather have you ask questions than find out after an assignment is complete that you didn't do it correctly because you were afraid to ask questions.

IN SUMMARY . . .

- As soon as you start a new job, be sure to learn the written and unwritten rules of the business.

- Showing up to work on time is one of the most important rules of the workplace.

- If you have a question or complaint, be sure to take it up with your immediate superior.

- Schedules are created to give your workday order and purpose.

- Coworkers may gossip, form cliques, or engage in other forms of office politics. This behavior should be carefully avoided, especially as a new employee.

8

LEARNING TO GO THE EXTRA MILE

A good employee is willing to go the extra mile, putting in extra effort to get the job done. Your boss should take notice if you're the one who volunteers to take on the extra work or if you're willing to stay late to finish an important project.

"It was the day of our office awards banquet, and everyone was heading out to the banquet hall for dinner," recalls Caroline. "The boss discovered that an entire file had not been fact-checked, and it was scheduled to go out to the printer at 5:00 P.M. I volunteered to miss the banquet and stay behind to check the document. My boss showed her gratitude by giving me Friday off. I made a big impression on her."

Going the extra mile is what makes a good employee move up in the company. Bosses may call it "hustle" or a "go-for-it attitude." They may consider the employee who's willing to do extra work their "go-to person." Bosses depend on these outstanding workers

✔ TRUE OR FALSE?

Are You Willing to Go the Extra Mile?

1. It doesn't matter if I make the extra effort at work; I'll never get promoted.

2. Employers must pay overtime to all employees.

Test yourself as you read through this chapter. The answers appear on page 82.

and often reward them with good assignments, pay raises, and promotions.

This is the equivalent of being the student in the class who does work for extra credit and earns straight As. The harder you work, the more your boss will see you as an outstanding employee.

David and Ben work at a record store. Kate, their manager, is thinking of promoting one of them, so she's watching them carefully to decide which one she'll choose.

David is always on time. He's friendly to the customers and willing to look in the back of the store for obscure CDs a customer may want. Kate has had to remind him to go take his lunch break, since he's so busy that he's lost track of the time.

Ben, on the other hand, just hands the customers what they ask for, never bothering to look in the back of the store if he can't find a title right away. He's always looking at his watch, impatient to go home. When Kate asked both of them, "Who's in the mood to rearrange the front display?" Ben rolled his eyes, but David agreed to do the job.

When the time came to award the promotion, the decision was easy: David was the hands-down winner.

Going the extra mile is what makes a good employee move up in the company.

OVERTIME

For an employee who is paid an hourly rate, any time worked in excess of 40 hours during a work-week is defined as *overtime*. Many workers *like* to work overtime so they can make more money. Let's

✍ EXERCISE

Here are a few examples of going the extra mile. Can you think of any others?

- Coming in early to stay on top of a big workload

- Staying at work late to get work done

- Being willing to do something over again if it wasn't right the first time

- Taking computer tutorials

- Volunteering to take on more work

say Mary is scheduled to work eight hours a day, five days a week. That adds up to 40 hours. If, on two evenings that week, Mary's boss asks her to stay and work an extra hour, Mary has worked 42 hours and has earned two hours of overtime. In many offices, factories, and stores, overtime is rewarded with *time-and-a-half,* which means workers can earn 1.5 times what they would normally earn in an hour. So if Mary usually earns $6 an hour, she would earn $9 for each hour she worked overtime.

A little more persistence, a little more effort, and what seemed hopeless failure may turn to glorious success.

—Elbert Hubbard, American writer, editor, and publisher

Many employees—and even some employers—don't know the law when it comes to overtime, and it's no wonder. For one thing, overtime laws can vary from state to state. For another, federal law (the Fair Labor Standards Act) divides employees into two categories: exempt and nonexempt. Employers are only obliged by law to pay overtime to nonexempt employees.

Nonexempt employees are all workers who are paid on an hourly basis and who put in more than 40 hours in a single workweek. Nonexempt employees must be paid overtime at time-and-a-half.

The company's executives, managers, and professional employees are almost always considered exempt. So are certain legally specified professions such as teachers, outside salespeople, and farm workers. Of course, many employees fall into a gray area between these two categories, which is where overtime regulation can get complicated.

Administrative employees hired on a monthly or annual salary basis are not always covered by state or federal overtime laws. Many employers consider these salaried employees to be professionals and expect them to put in extra time to get work done. However, many of these employers still try to make it up to employees who work extra hours by offering extra time off, sometimes called compensation time.

If you're a salaried employee and are not sure whether you fall into the exempt or nonexempt category, ask your supervisor or someone in your company's personnel office. If you're afraid to ask, contact the nearest office of your state's labor department. If you're employed on a salaried basis, it's probably not smart to complain if you have to put in a few extra hours once every few months. But if it happens week after week, your employer may be taking unfair advantage of you and violating the law.

WORK HOURS AND JOB LIMITATIONS

The Fair Labor Standards Act sets limitations on the hours young people may work. Here are the basic rules:

SURF THE WEB: FAIR LABOR STANDARDS ACT

elaws: Fair Labor Standards Act Advisor
http://www.dol.gov/elaws/flsa.htm

U.S. Department of Labor: Employment Standards Administration
http://www.dol.gov/esa/whd/flsa

Youth Rules!
http://www.youthrules.dol.gov

- If you're 18 or older, your work hours are unlimited in accordance with minimum wage and overtime requirements.

- If you're 16 or 17, you may work unlimited hours at any nonhazardous job.

- If you're 14 or 15, you may work outside school hours in a nonhazardous job up to:

  - three hours on a school day

  - 18 hours in a school week

  - eight hours on a nonschool day

  - 40 hours on a nonschool week

- Work must be performed between 7:00 A.M. and 7:00 P.M., except from June 1 through Labor Day, when evening hours may extend to 9:00 P.M.

JOBS THAT ARE PROHIBITED FOR TEENS

If you're under 18, the Fair Labor Standards Act says you cannot work in jobs with these elements:

- Manufacturing and storing of explosives
- Driving a motor vehicle and being an outside helper on a motor vehicle
- Coal mining
- Logging and sawmilling
- Power-driven woodworking machines
- Exposure to radioactive substances
- Power-driven hoisting apparatus
- Power-driven metal-forming, punching, and shearing machines
- Mining, other than coal mining
- Meat packing or processing (including the use of power-driven meat slicing machines)
- Power-driven bakery machines
- Power-driven paper-product machines
- Manufacturing brick, tile, and related products
- Power-driven circular saws, band saws, and guillotine shears
- Wrecking, demolition, and shipbreaking operations
- Roofing operations and all work on or about a roof
- Excavation operations

✔ TRUE OR FALSE: ANSWERS

Are You Willing to Go the Extra Mile?

1. It doesn't matter if I make the extra effort at work; I'll never get promoted.

False. Your extra effort may or may not help you get promoted, but it will make you stand out in the workplace. Bosses appreciate workers who are willing to make the extra effort to improve a product, make a customer happy, or help a work team meet a deadline.

2. Employers must pay overtime to all employees.

False. Employees who are paid at an hourly rate who work more than 40 hours a week are eligible for overtime pay. Salaried employees who work more than 40 hours a week usually do not receive overtime pay, but may be offered compensatory time, extra time off the job.

IN SUMMARY . . .

- A good employee is willing to put in extra hours to get the job done—and a good boss will notice and compensate the worker with time off, pay, or even a promotion.

- Working overtime is often expected of salaried workers.

- For nonexempt workers who are paid by the hour, any work exceeding 40 hours a week is considered overtime and deserves time-and-a-half compensation.
- The Fair Labor Standards Act is in place to protect the rights of nonexempt employees and to ensure that they are compensated for overtime.

9

DEALING WITH COWORKERS

You know it's important that you get along with your teachers, your coaches, and your parents. These are the people who have authority over your life. They make major decisions that affect you, so getting along with them is an advantage to you.

It's the same with your bosses. Establishing a good rapport with the people in charge of your schedule, responsibilities, and general working atmosphere means that you'll always be given a higher level of respect—and possibly a break or favor when you need one.

"I get along with my boss fine," says Sheila of her supervisor at her management job. "Sometimes it's difficult because he can be a bit annoying. But I just keep in mind that he's the guy in charge and my job is to listen to him. Some other people in the office don't like him, and they don't even try to get along with him. He senses that, and they clash. Since he and

✔ TRUE OR FALSE?

How Are Your People Skills?

1. It's important to respect my boss—even if he or she doesn't seem to like me.

2. I will become friends with every one of my coworkers.

3. It's important to be diplomatic with coworkers, but sometimes trying to get along just won't work.

Test yourself as you read through this chapter. The answers appear on pages 92–93.

I have a good rapport, he gives me good assignments and is more willing to consider giving me a day off.

"Plus," Sheila adds, "my evaluation reports are always excellent."

It's also important to get along with your coworkers. You've read about office politics. Being polite can be a challenge when a particularly mean-spirited colleague gives you and everybody else a hard time. You want your office to be a pleasant environment. You want to be able to do your work efficiently, free from the kinds of battles and unspoken negative attitudes that make school so difficult sometimes. You have to work with the people around you, joining with them to cooperate on projects or depending on them for important contributions. As a result, it's most advantageous if you and your coworkers just get along.

It's most advantageous if you and your coworkers just get along.

Neither province, parish, nor nation, neighborhood, family, nor individual, can live profitably in exclusion from the rest of the world.

—Ralph Tyler Flewelling, American philosopher

WHAT DO I DO IF PEOPLE DON'T LIKE ME?

"Act professionally," says security supervisor Ron Naylor. "You can be friendly with your coworkers

---

SURF THE WEB: BE NICE TO YOUR BOSS

About.com: Getting Along with Your Boss and Co-Workers
  http://careerplanning.about.com/od/
    bosscoworkers/Getting_Along_With_Your_Boss_
    and_CoWorkers.htm

First30Days: How to Handle a New Boss
  http://www.first30days.com/starting-a-new-job/
    articles/how-to-handle-a-new-boss.html#

SeekingSuccess.com: Getting Along with Your Boss
  http://www.seekingsuccess.com/articles/art103.php

Yahoo! HotJobs: Getting on the Boss's Good Side
  http://hotjobs.yahoo.com/career-articles-getting_
    on_the_boss_s_good_side-498

Getting along and communicating well with coworkers is especially important for those working in hospitals and other high-stakes job settings. (David M. Grossman, The Image Works)

without being friends with them. It's all a part of diplomacy, and that's a vital element of a successful workplace."

Diplomacy is the practice of tactfully dealing with other people so that you can work together peacefully. You've probably heard about diplomacy between countries. It's usually mentioned when negotiators meet to come to a decision or to achieve a shared goal with compromise and respect. Country leaders often must put aside their personal differences and work together as partners. That's what you must do in the office.

Unfortunately, there will be times when diplomacy is just not going to be possible. These are the rare occasions when the working atmosphere is so unpleasant, or a coworker is unwilling to compromise or be diplomatic, that there is no other choice but to take a complaint up the chain of command.

Communication is important in the workplace because you need to help reduce a patient's fear during an exam and let your coworkers know what you need.

—Michelle Scoglietti, radiologic technologist and continuing education reviewer for the American Society of Radiologic Technologists

"We had this one editor named Sally when I worked for a newspaper," says Chris, a sports editor. "She was just a miserable person, snapping at us and being downright mean whenever any of us made a mistake. She obviously hated her job, and she wanted us to hate ours, too. We all tried our best to work with her, ignoring her comments and trying to rise above her level. But it was just impossible.

"We wound up having to go to the executive editor with our complaints," Chris continues. "We told him that Sally had just made the editorial office a miserable place to be, and that we were having trouble getting our work done. The executive editor listened to our complaints and took action by reprimanding Sally. When Sally's behavior worsened, she was moved out of our office."

If you can't get along with someone after you've done everything you can to diplomatically remedy the problem on your own, someone else has to step in to fix the situation.

In this instance, the workplace is not that different from school. If you can't get along with someone after you've done everything you can to diplomatically remedy the problem on your own, someone else has to step in to fix the situation.

COMMON QUESTIONS

Q. **I've tried to be nice, but one coworker just isn't nice to me. What do I do?**

A. There's nothing you can do, except to act professionally. Act as if this person does like you, and just deal with him or her when necessary. Do not be mean back to him or her.

Q. **My boss doesn't seem to like me. She never smiles at me and never says hello. What do I do?**

A. Maybe your boss does like you. It's possible that he or she is just extremely busy, as most bosses are, and feels pressured to have a friendly conversation with you by the water cooler.

If your boss is just not nice to you, it's time to be diplomatic. Treat the boss with the appropriate amount of respect due to anyone's boss, do your job to the best of your ability, and deal with him or her in a professional manner.

Q. **My coworker asks me to cover for her while she goes out during work hours to meet her boyfriend. What do I do?**

A. Here's where diplomacy gets tricky. On the one hand, you want to be friendly with this coworker

HOW TO DEAL WITH OTHERS SUCCESSFULLY

- Always speak with respect.

- Always be considerate of others.

- Give the benefit of the doubt. (Maybe they're having a hard day.)

- Treat others as you would want to be treated.

- Be professional.

- Always be willing to compromise.

- Keep the lines of communication open. Be willing to talk it out.

- Act according to your position. Don't try to boss around the boss.

- Don't participate in office gossip or mean-spiritedness.

- Be friendly.

- Be appreciative when others go out of their way to help you.

and do her a favor. But this favor could get both of you fired if the truth comes out. Since honesty is always the best policy, you should tell your friend that lying to the boss would make you very uncomfortable and suggest that she ask the boss for a 10-minute break now in exchange for working 10 minutes extra after quitting time. Most bosses are pretty reasonable if they think you're playing straight with them.

Coworkers often help each other out in small ways, but never allow a coworker to put you into a position of lying to the boss or violating company rules—at least not if you value your job.

✔ TRUE OR FALSE?

How Are Your People Skills?

1. It's important to respect my boss—even if he or she doesn't seem to like me.

True. You should always treat your boss with respect. But don't jump to the conclusion that your boss doesn't like you—he or she may just be very busy, under a lot of pressure, or simply have a reserved personality. Whether your boss likes you or not, it's important to keep him or her happy. See "Get on Your Boss's Good Side" in chapter 3 for a few useful tips.

2. I will become friends with every one of my coworkers.

False. Your main goal at work is to complete the tasks assigned to you by your supervisor, not to make friends. You will develop respectful, productive, and sometimes even warm relationships with your coworkers, but that doesn't mean you will necessarily become friends with everyone.

3. It's important to be diplomatic with coworkers, but sometimes trying to get along just won't work.

True. Not everyone wants to get along in the workplace. Some of your coworkers may even go out of their way to make your life miserable. If you encounter such a situation, you need to bring the issue to your manager's attention.

IN SUMMARY . . .

- To make the workplace an efficient and pleasant environment, it is critical to get along with your coworkers and supervisors.

- When problems between you and a coworker or boss arise, use diplomacy to try to resolve the situation quickly.

- If a problem can't be solved using diplomatic means, take it up with your immediate boss.

PART III

Your Rights and Obligations as an Employee

10

YOUR PERSONAL RIGHTS AS AN EMPLOYEE

As an employee, certain rights are guaranteed to you under law. This means that certain conditions must be met by your employer in order to provide a safe and comfortable working atmosphere for all personnel.

DISCRIMINATION AND HARASSMENT

First and foremost, under law, you may not be a victim of discrimination. *Discrimination* is the unlawful practice of treating people with disrespect or disfavor because of their race, age, gender, religion, or certain other factors of their lifestyles. Laws are in place to prevent discrimination in the workplace. You may lodge a complaint with your superiors if you feel you are a victim of discrimination.

You also have a right to be free from *sexual harassment*. Your coworkers or bosses should never make

✔ TRUE OR FALSE?

Do You Know Your Personal Rights as an Employee?

1. Discrimination is the unlawful practice of treating people with disrespect and disfavor because of their gender.

2. It's my legal obligation to report sexual harassment.

3. It's okay to laugh at the new guy's funny accent.

Test yourself as you read through this chapter. The answers appear on pages 103–104.

unwanted sexual advances or contact with you. They should also not contribute to an uncomfortable or hostile working environment by telling sexually explicit jokes, distributing suggestive materials, or treating you as a sex object. Most sexual harassment is done by men to women, but men get harassed by women, and members of the same sex harass each other. According to the Equal Employment Opportunity Commission (EEOC), men constituted 16 percent of all sexual harassment cases filed in fiscal year 2007.

You could be found guilty for not reporting harassment against coworkers.

It's your legal obligation to report sexual harassment. In fact, you could be found guilty for not reporting harassment against coworkers if you are aware the harassment exists but do nothing about it.

SURF THE WEB: FIGHT BACK AGAINST WORKPLACE DISCRIMINATION AND HARASSMENT

Equality and Human Rights Commission
http://www.equalityhumanrights.com

Equal Employment Opportunity Commission
http://www.eeoc.gov

Harassment Hotline Inc.
http://www.end-harassment.com

Women's Rights at Work
http://www.citizenactionny.org

WorkRelationships Inc.
http://www.workrelationships.com

If harassed in any way, you should first tell the offender that you do not welcome the comments or actions and that you'd appreciate it if he or she would act appropriately around you.

☛ FACT

Title VII of the Civil Rights Act denotes that there are two categories of sexual harassment:

1. *Quid pro quo,* in which the conditions of employment, hiring, promotions, and retention are contingent on the victim providing sexual favors.

2. *Hostile working environment,* in which there is "discrimination, intimidation, ridicule and insult which is sufficiently severe or pervasive to alter the conditions of the victim's employment, and create an abusive working environment."

WHAT TO DO IF HARASSMENT DOESN'T STOP

If the harassment still doesn't stop, do the following:

1. Report the offender's behavior to your boss. It's your legal right to do so, and getting your boss involved is the only way to stop the offensive behavior, as well as ensure that an official record of the harassment has been made.

2. If the harassment continues, file a formal charge of harassment with the Equal Employment Opportunity Commission. Visit its Web site, http://www.eeoc.gov, for more information.

SAFE WORKING CONDITIONS

You also have a right to safe and healthy working conditions. Your office should be heated in the winter and comfortable in the summer. There should

USEFUL RESOURCES

The EEOC offers a variety of publications about discrimination and sexual harassment at its Web site, http://www.eeoc.gov/publications.html. Many are available for download; others are available as print publications.

be fire exits. It should be free from asbestos or any other contaminants that may harm your health or put you in danger in any way. Most offices are inspected for safety, and you have a right to expect that you are safe in your workplace.

☞ FACT

According to the Occupational Safety and Health Administration (OSHA), in 2005, work injuries and illness rates dropped to their lowest level— 4.6 cases per 100 workers—since the U.S. began collecting this information.

See OSHA's Web site, http://www.osha.gov, for more information.

DECENCY AND RESPECT

Finally, you have a right to be treated with *decency.* You are a person, not a slave, and no one in your workplace should belittle you as a person.

HOW TWO WORKERS STOOD UP FOR THEIR RIGHTS

When Anthony started his job as an assistant in an architect's office, he was nervous about fitting in. So he laughed when the other architects made fun of his accent and his appearance. He thought that was how he would become "one of the guys." Over time though, the comments hurt his feelings. He had a right to be treated with decency, so he asked

BOOKS ABOUT DISCRIMINATION OR HARASSMENT IN THE WORKPLACE

Boland, Mary. *Sexual Harassment in the Workplace.* Naperville, Ill.: Sphinx Publishing, 2005.

Gregory, Raymond F. *Unwelcome and Unlawful: Sexual Harassment in the American Workplace.* Ithaca, N.Y.: Cornell University Press, 2004.

Howard, Linda Gordon. *The Sexual Harassment Handbook.* Franklin Lakes, N.J.: Career Press, 2007.

Kaip, Sarah. *The Woman's Workplace Survival Guide.* Medford, Oreg.: Advantage Source, 2005.

Levy, Anne C., and Michele A. Paludi. *Workplace Sexual Harassment.* 2d ed. Upper Saddle River, N.J.: Prentice Hall, 2001.

his coworkers to lay off the jokes. They did, and he no longer dreads going to work.

Every time Carrie Ann had to pass the office door of one of her supervisors, she'd hear him whistle at her. She just smiled uncomfortably and continued on her way. He was her supervisor, after all. Soon he was telling her that she had a nice body. He even told her that she would look good in shorter skirts. Knowing that this was inappropriate behavior for anyone in the office—especially a supervisor—Carrie Ann asked him to stop making those types of comments. She told him that she didn't like his inappropriate statements and that if he kept harassing her, she would bring her complaint to his boss. The supervisor apologized and stopped immediately.

✔ TRUE OR FALSE: ANSWERS

Do You Know Your Personal Rights as an Employee?

1. Discrimination is the unlawful practice of treating people with disrespect and disfavor because of their gender.

Partially true. In addition to gender, peoples can be discriminated against because of their race, age, religion, and certain other factors of their lifestyles. All discrimination is wrong and illegal under U.S. federal law.

2. It's my legal obligation to report sexual harassment.

True. You could face legal action if you have knowledge of sexual harassment, but don't report it.

3. It's okay to laugh at the new guy's funny accent.

False. This is just one example of insensitive behavior that is unacceptable in the workplace. Try to find common ground that helps you build respectful and productive relationships with coworkers from different ethnic, religious, or social backgrounds.

IN SUMMARY . . .

- You have the right to work in an environment that is free of discrimination and sexual harassment.

- Your workplace should be clean and safe.

- As a human being, you deserve to be treated with decency by all coworkers and supervisors.

- Laws are in place to protect your rights. If you feel that any of your rights have been violated, act in this order: Confront the offender, address the issue with your supervisor, or, as a last measure, take it up in the courts.

11

YOUR FINANCIAL RIGHTS AS AN EMPLOYEE

Finally, it's payday. Depending on how your company distributes money, you'll either get paid weekly, every two weeks, or once a month. There are several things you should keep in mind before receiving your first paycheck.

PAYCHECK DEDUCTIONS

When you get your first paycheck, you might be a little surprised. "Wait a minute!" you cry when you see the total of the check: $179.37. "I worked 40 hours this week. At $6 an hour, I should have $240 here!" Money is missing from your check. But it hasn't been stolen. It's been *deducted* from your check to pay for taxes and insurance.

Your paycheck will look different from the preceding one. You may have different deductions or additional amounts withheld from your paycheck.

✔ TRUE OR FALSE?

Do You Know Your Financial Rights as an Employee?

1. It's important to study my pay stub each pay period to ensure that it does not contain errors.

2. It's okay to use a sick day if I simply don't feel like going to work.

3. Participating in a 401(k) plan will help me save for retirement.

Test yourself as you read through this chapter. The answers appear on pages 115–116.

The deductions presented in this model are explained as follows:

- The amount of *federal income tax* taken from your check depends on your salary, tax filing status, etc., and is paid directly to the Internal Revenue Service.

- *F.I.C.A. (Federal Insurance Contributions Act) tax* goes to Social Security and Medicare, which you will use for your income and health insurance when you are too old to work or if you become disabled. Your employer has paid an equal amount as its contribution. (Medicare contributions are listed separately on some paychecks.)

STATEMENT OF EARNINGS

Name: Jones, Jefferson

ENTITLEMENTS	DEDUCTIONS	YEAR TO DATE
		Gross $1,920.00
Basic Salary: $240.00	Federal: $28.35	$226.80
	FICA: $18.36	$146.88
	State: $.07	$.56
	SDI: $2.48	$19.84
	Health: $11.37	$90.96
Total: $240.00	$60.63	NET PAY (WEEK): $179.37
		YTD: $1,434.96

- *State income tax* is paid directly to your state.

- *SDI (State Disability Insurance) tax* is paid by residents of California, Hawaii, New Jersey, New York, Puerto Rico, and Rhode Island in order to provide benefits if you are temporarily disabled by a nonwork illness or injury.

- *Health insurance* is included on your paycheck if your company offers group medical and dental benefits. This is your share of the cost to maintain your insurance coverage.

In the end, of the $240 Jefferson Jones earned, he takes home $179.37, which is known as his *net pay.*

☞ FACT

Always check your paycheck for errors. Keep your own record of the hours you have worked, and check it against your earnings statement. It's up to you to ensure that you receive the correct salary and benefits payments!

VACATION TIME

Companies have their own policies regarding vacation time. If you need to take a few vacation days for a sports tournament or a wedding out of state, you'll have to request a few days off ahead of time. Some employers prefer that you make the request days or even weeks in advance and that you put it in writing for your supervisor.

"It's very important to know what your company's policies are," says Steven, a production assistant. "Some companies don't allow you to take a vacation until you've been with them for a certain amount of time, like four or six months."

The vast majority of American companies offer paid vacation time, but some employers only provide time off without pay. Be sure you know what applies at your workplace.

AVERAGE NUMBER OF VACATION DAYS OFFERED TO WORKERS BY COUNTRY

Country	# of Days
Italy	42
France	37
Germany	35
Brazil	34
United Kingdom	28
Canada	26
Korea	25
Japan	25
United States	13

Source: World Tourism Organization/ InfoPlease.com

Holiday schedules depend on the decisions of management.

HOLIDAYS

You should be informed about which holidays you'll have off from work. Your supervisor is likely to give you a list of days off. If not, inquire about your schedule. Depending on the type of business you work for, you may have to work on some national holidays. For example, most restaurants stay open on Thanksgiving. Some executive offices stay open on holidays as well. Holiday schedules depend on the decisions of management. If you need a day off because of a religious holiday, be sure to tell your supervisor well in advance.

SICK DAYS

Companies also have their own policies regarding sick days. Many workers have an allotment of sick days (perhaps 10 a year, or one a month), and it is from this number that sick days may be taken. So if you have the flu and you just can't make it to work, you'll have to use one of your sick days. Some government agencies and some unionized companies allow their workers to treat the sick days they are allotted as days they are entitled to take off whether they are sick or not.

Most private employers believe sick days should not be used unless you are genuinely too sick to work. Managers in such companies frown on workers who always manage to be sick for exactly as many days each year as they have sick leave. In fact, they think of them as cheating the company out of money. When you are too sick to work, always notify your supervisor as early in the day as possible.

PERSONAL DAYS

A *personal day* is one that you take off from work for your own reasons. Perhaps you have a doctor's appointment or you have to travel out of town for a wedding. Use this personal day to take care of any outside business you have to do. Some companies offer one or more personal days a year; others do not offer them at all.

Look at your company's benefits package to be sure you're getting—and using—all the benefits your company offers.

BENEFITS

Your job may offer *full benefits*. But what does that mean? To you, holding a job may be a benefit in itself, in that you now have money for college, money to buy clothes, and some experience in your chosen field. But that's not what the term benefits means.

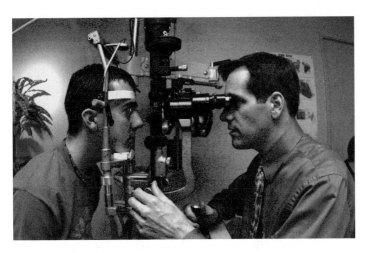

Optometric insurance is just one fringe benefit that your employer may offer in addition to salary. (Roy Willey, The Daily Courier/AP Photo)

Benefits are the special elements that come with a job. Some benefits are full medical and dental coverage, a retirement plan, tuition reimbursement (your company helps pay your school costs), or profit sharing (you get a small percentage of the company's profits). Many workers look for such excellent benefits when they apply for jobs. Look at your company's benefits package to be sure you're getting—and using—all the benefits your company offers.

ASKING QUESTIONS

Who do you go to when you have a question about your paycheck or your benefits? Ask your supervisor to direct you to a person in the accounting or human resources department who handles these questions.

WHAT TO DO WITH YOUR PAYCHECK

When you get your paycheck, you may be tempted to spend every penny. But that's not a wise move. You can spend some of the money and allow the rest to grow in savings or investments. Here are a few options for where to stash your cash:

- A *savings account* allows your money to accumulate interest over time, for as long as you keep it in the account.

- A *checking account* allows you to access money by writing a check or using a debit

SURF THE WEB: MONEY-SAVING TIPS

eHow: How to Save Money
http://www.ehow.com/how_2256041_
save-money.html

Debt-Proof Living
http://www.cheapskatemonthly.com

The Motley Fool
http://www.fool.com

SavingAdvice.com
http://www.savingadvice.com

SavingSecrets
http://www.savingsecrets.com

66 Ways to Save Money
http://www.pueblo.gsa.gov/cic_text/
money/66ways/content

YoungInvestor.com
http://www.younginvestor.com

card. Some checking accounts also offer minimal interest.

- Use direct deposit if you want to be sure your money goes straight into the bank.

You won't have to take your check to the bank, stand in line, or fill out deposit slips.

- Know your *investment options.* Research savings bonds, certificates of deposit (known as CDs), mutual funds, stocks, etc. Remember that while mutual funds and stocks may give you a higher percentage return on your money, they also entail higher risk.

- *Employer-sponsored savings* is a smart option if your company offers workers the chance to buy stock in the company through small payroll deductions. Other employer saving plans include *401(k) plans,* which are named after a section of the federal tax code. These plans allow you to save money for retirement. Money is taken out *before* taxes are deducted. (In other words, you don't pay taxes on this money until you use it years later.) Some companies match all or part of what employees save in 401(k) accounts. Unless you need to spend every penny you earn, you should take advantage of such tax-deferred, company-assisted savings programs.

✔ TRUE OR FALSE: ANSWERS

Do You Know Your Financial Rights as an Employee?

1. It's important to study my pay stub each pay period to ensure that it does not contain errors.

True. Always check your pay stub to ensure that your pay is correct, that the appropriate amount of taxes have been deducted, and to make sure that there are no other errors. If you find an error, bring it to the attention of your supervisor.

2. It's okay to use a sick day if I simply don't feel like going to work.

True or false depending on the employer. As a general rule, you should try to save your sick days for when you're actually sick. Some government agencies and unionized companies allow workers to use sick days whether they are sick or not, but private companies typically frown on workers who use a sick day to go to a ballgame, extend their vacation to Hawaii, or take a day off for some other non-illness-related reason.

3. Participating in a 401(k) plan will help me save for retirement.

True. Many larger companies offer 401(k) plans, which allow workers to save for retirement.

Money deposited in 401(k) accounts is not taxed until you cash out the account. Some companies even match all or part of what you save in a 401(k) program. Visit http://www.irs.gov/taxtopics/tc424.html for more information.

IN SUMMARY . . .

- The money you earn on your job is yours, *after* taxes.

- When you plan to take vacation days off, be sure to put it in writing and give your supervisor plenty of notice so he or she can cover for you while you're gone.

- Most businesses give employees certain days off during the year as holidays. These days vary depending on where you work, so request a holiday schedule when you start a new job.

- Sick days are there for a purpose: Use them when you're legitimately sick, not simply when you want days off.

- Your company may also offer personal days; use them for personal business such as doctor appointments.

- The money you earn is yours, so manage it wisely. Take advantage of savings, investment, and retirement accounts to put away money for your future.

PART IV

Troubleshooting

12

RESOLVING PROBLEMS

Every employee has an occasional bad day at the office. Mistakes are made, personalities clash, and everything seems more overwhelming than usual. Over the course of their careers, the best employees learn how to deal with problems before they become big obstacles.

RECOGNIZING THE SEVERITY OF THE PROBLEM

Whenever a problem arises, your first step should be to ask: Is this problem a simple misunderstanding? Most problems in the office are just that. Directions may have been unclear; maybe someone thought the deadline was the next day, or a name was left off the mailing list. A problem that results from a simple misunderstanding should end with a quick remedy to the problem. Then you should move on. Brooding, complaining, or pointing fingers to blame the guilty party is a waste of time.

A problem that results from a simple misunderstanding should end with a quick remedy.

119

✔ TRUE OR FALSE?

Do You Know How to Resolve Problems?

1. Most problems in the workplace stem from simple misunderstandings.

2. When a problem with a coworker cannot be resolved, you should consider leaving the company.

3. If you make a mistake at work, it's important to admit it, fix it, and move on.

Test yourself as you read through this chapter. The answers appear on pages 123–124.

In the whole round of human affairs, little is so fatal to peace as misunderstanding.

—Margaret E. Sangster, American author

Perhaps the problem is not so easily explained. "A coworker and I just had a personality conflict. We just didn't see eye-to-eye on anything, and we did not get along," explains Gina, an insurance claims adjustor. "The only solution was just to stay out of each other's way, be cordial whenever we did see each other and just peacefully coexist in the office."

A personality conflict is obviously not an easy problem to solve. Sometimes two people just cannot get along. But Gina's approach worked fine; she and her coworker were able to go about their business in a peaceful way, avoiding conflict.

SMART CONFRONTATIONS

Let's assume peaceful coexistence is not working between you and another coworker. It's time for the two of you to sit down and work the problem out before the tension between you gets in the way of your work.

- Ask the other person if you can talk. Schedule a time that's good for both of you.

- Understand that you and your coworker cannot change your personalities, but that you'll just have to come up with some ground rules for mutual respect.

- Don't be hostile. A friendly approach is best.

- Only deal with the issue at hand; don't drag up ancient history. Be specific about your complaints, and work to solve the particular problem.

- Discuss your ideas objectively. It's not a contest to see whose idea is better.

- Don't make demands.

- State clearly that you want to work this out and that you want to be able to work together in peace.

- Most important, compromise.

WHEN TO SEEK HELP

• When you're unable to solve a problem on your own

• When you feel your rights are not being respected

• When you feel unsafe at work

• When you feel the offender will respond to someone with more authority

But what happens when a problem is completely unresolvable through your own diplomacy and compromise? In these (hopefully rare) cases, you need to take the issue up the "chain of command." Discuss the problem with your supervisor first, and if that does not lead to a solution, ask the supervisor for a referral upward to the manager. Take whatever steps are necessary to solve a conflict in the workplace.

Act professionally, accept assistance, and work with others to reach the goal.

Now assume that you caused the problem. "I felt terrible after I made a big mistake in the office," says Tom. "But an older coworker with more experience told me something that put it all in perspective. He said, 'Everyone makes mistakes. It's how we learn. Sure, you may get in trouble, but a true professional accepts the blame, fixes the problem, and moves on.'"

You will make mistakes. A key ingredient in moving past a problem is the use of diplomacy. Act professionally, accept assistance, and work with others to reach the goal. Appeal to more experienced coworkers to share their knowledge with you. Learn the lesson it takes in order to avoid repeating the mistake.

✔ TRUE OR FALSE: ANSWERS

Do You Know How to Resolve Problems?

1. Most problems in the workplace stem from simple misunderstandings.

True. Simple miscommunication or human error causes most workplace problems. Once you identify the problem, it's important to find a solution and resist the urge to assign blame or brood about the issue.

2. When a problem with a coworker cannot be resolved, you should consider leaving the company.

False. If you've unsuccessfully tried to resolve a problem with your coworker, you should take it up the "chain of command." First, ask your supervisor for help. If that doesn't solve the problem, ask your supervisor to refer you to his or her manager. Do whatever it takes to solve the problem. Don't let problems with a coworker chase you away from a job you like.

3. If you make a mistake at work, it's important to admit it, fix it, and move on.

True. Everyone makes mistakes, and the key to earning respect in the workplace is to admit your mistake, accept guidance from your boss or coworkers on how to remedy the issue, and move on. Avoid making the same mistake twice.

IN SUMMARY . . .

- When a problem arises, first determine if it is indeed a problem or simply just a misunderstanding.

- If you're faced with a personality conflict with a coworker, either try to work around the problem or confront it peacefully.

- Finally, if diplomacy and compromise don't work, ask for assistance from your next superior in the chain of command.

- If it is *you* who have made a mistake, don't dwell on it. Fix it yourself or ask for help; then move on.

13

ASKING FOR
A RAISE

Charlie had the same job for over a year. His boss was happy with his work, and he had many repeat customers. Charlie was doing a great job.

"You know," Charlie thought, "I've been here a while, making the same amount I was making when I was new. I think I deserve a raise."

Charlie's right. Based on his performance and the relationships he's built over the past year, he does deserve a raise. So he makes an appointment with his boss.

"What is it you wanted to talk to me about, Charlie?" asked his boss, Terry.

"I've been in this position for a year, and I think I'm doing a pretty good job," Charlie said.

"You are doing a very good job," Terry agreed.

"I'm glad you agree. In that case, I hope you'll consider giving me a raise," Charlie said, remembering not to *demand* a raise, but to ask with respect.

✔ **TRUE OR FALSE?**

Do You Know How to Ask for a Raise?

1. If you think you deserve a raise, you should demand it from your boss.

2. When asking for a raise, it's a good idea to conduct research to support your opinion.

3. It's important to consider the overall financial health of your company when deciding whether or not you should ask for a raise.

Test yourself as you read through this chapter. The answers appear on pages 133–134.

Terry thought for a moment, nodded his head, and said. "How does $9 an hour sound?"

Charlie was making $7.25 an hour. "Great," Charlie smiled. "Thank you."

"Thank you, and keep up the good work."

The key element in Charlie's scenario is that he *deserved* a raise. He had been doing a great job, and his boss thought so, too. If Charlie had been a slacker, if he never put forth extra effort, if he always showed up late, always complained, and never listened to his supervisors, he wouldn't have much hope of getting a raise and shouldn't have asked for one in the first place.

SURF THE WEB:
ASKING FOR A RAISE

About.com: How to Ask for a Raise
http://careerplanning.about.com/od/
negotiatingoffers/a/raise.htm

Forbes.com: Seven No-Nos When Asking For
a Raise
http://www.forbes.com/2006/01/04/
careers-work-employment-cx_
sr_0105bizbasics_print.html

PayScale.com: How to Make Money in a
Recession: Ask for a Raise
http://www.payscale.com/ask-for-a-
raise-during-recession

HOW DO YOU KNOW WHEN YOU DESERVE A RAISE?

Perhaps you've been in your job for a long time. Perhaps you've received plenty of praise from your coworkers and supervisors. Is that enough? What you need to do is assess your accomplishments. Use the questions that follow to evaluate your worthiness for a raise.

- How long have I been on the job?

- How many promotions have I had in this company since I got here?

- What are my job responsibilities?

- Do I do any work that is above my position (things that my superiors would usually do)?

- What special skills have I learned on the job (new computer programs, etc.)?

- Have I received praise or good performance reports recently?

- What examples can I offer to prove that I'm doing a good job?

Once you've assessed your worthiness, it's time to figure out just how *much* of a raise to expect. "I thought my salary would double," confessed Charlie. "But I guess that was a bit unrealistic. I'm happy with my $1.75-per-hour raise. At the end of the week, that's $70 more in my pocket. In time, I hope to get an even bigger raise."

It's up to your boss to decide the size of your raise, should you be granted one.

It's up to your boss to decide the size of your raise, should you be granted one. Think of it this way: You're asking for money, so you have to be gracious. Allow the boss to come up with the first figure on his or her own. If you choose, you can attempt to bargain up, but that takes a careful amount of business savvy and a friendly nature. You don't want to be too demanding.

DO YOU DESERVE A RAISE?

The following Web sites will provide you with salary information for starting, mid-range, and experienced workers in your field. This information will be useful when you ask for a raise.

Glassdoor.com
  http://www.glassdoor.com

JobStar Central
  http://jobstar.org

Nonprofit Salaries
  http://www.idealist.org/en/career/
    salarysurvey.html

Payscale.com
  http://www.salary.com

Salary.com
  http://www.salary.com

SalaryWebsite
  http://www.salarywebsite.com

U.S. Department of Labor: Salary Estimates
  http://www.salarysurvey.org

THE FIVE RULES OF ASKING FOR A RAISE

1. Schedule time with your boss. Don't just walk in and expect him or her to listen to you. Bosses are generally busy. (And if he or she is annoyed by your sudden entrance, you probably won't have a good chance of getting a raise.)

2. Be respectful.

3. Ask for a raise; don't demand one.

4. Don't whine. Saying, "But Julia got a raise, and I've been here longer!" isn't going to make the boss admire your approach.

5. Believe you deserve a raise. Walking into the boss's office with a calm, cool air of confidence shows that you believe you're deserving of the raise and maybe a promotion, too.

"I don't mind if an employee wants to push for more money," says John, a partner in a law firm. "It shows he believes in himself, and he's willing to go for what he deserves. It has to be done the right way, though. I don't like it when some beginner comes in here and tries to push me around. That's the quickest way I know how *not* to get a raise."

DON'T FORGET TO CONSIDER FRINGE BENEFITS

When deciding if you should ask for a raise, don't forget to factor in the quality of your fringe benefits (such as health insurance, vacation and sick days allotted, profit-sharing plan, etc.). Some companies provide excellent benefits, which may offset your low salary.

If you ask for a raise, but are turned down, you should consider trying to negotiate for improved benefits. Your employer may be more willing to grant you a few extra perks, rather than set a precedent by awarding raises. Some of the fringe benefits that you might ask to receive include bonuses for meeting project deadlines, use of a company car, use of a company mobile phone, the ability to telecommute, flexible schedule, reimbursement for continuing education, medical insurance, dental insurance, optical insurance, profit sharing, vacation time, and change in job title.

RAISES AND COMPANY PERFORMANCE

There's one more point to consider before asking for a raise: How is the company doing? If business has been terrible, the boss may not be able to afford to give you, or anyone, a raise, even if you've been doing an excellent job. You may not always know for sure whether business is good or bad, but you should be able to pick up hints from what's going on around you. Has everyone been asked to cut back on supplies lately? Do managers often look tense and worried? Is the company slow in paying its bills?

Almost all businesses have ups and downs. If you ask for a raise when things are in the pits, not only

BOOKS ON SALARY NEGOTIATION

Chapman, Jack. *Negotiating Your Salary: How to Make $1,000 A Minute.* 5th ed. Berkeley, Calif.: Ten Speed Press, 2006.

DeLuca, Matthew J., and Nanette F. DeLuca. *Perfect Phrases for Negotiating Salary and Job Offers: Hundreds of Ready-to-Use Phrases to Help You Get the Best Possible Salary, Perks or Promotion.* New York: McGraw-Hill, 2006.

Krannich, Ron. *Give Me More Money!: Smart Salary Negotiation Tips for Getting Paid What You're Really Worth.* Manassas Park, Va.: Impact Publications, 2008.

Wegerbauer, Maryanne. *Next-Day Salary Negotiation: Prepare Tonight to Get Your Best Pay Tomorrow (Help in a Hurry).* Indianapolis, Ind.: JIST Works, 2007.

are you unlikely to get it, but the boss may conclude you are oblivious to the business's problems or just don't care about them. In business, timing can mean everything. Sometimes it's smart to wait for the right moment—such as right after the boss comes in smiling after landing a lucrative new contract.

In business, timing can mean everything.

✔ TRUE OR FALSE: ANSWERS

Do You Know How to Ask for a Raise?

1. If you think you deserve a raise, you should demand it from your boss.

False. Demanding a raise will get you nowhere with your boss. You need to respectfully request a raise if you believe you deserve one.

2. When asking for a raise, it's a good idea to conduct research to support your opinion.

True. Gather as much research as possible to help convince your manager that you deserve a raise. This might include statistics on the average pay for workers with your education level and work experience or information on the time and money you saved the company due to new programs or procedures you created.

3. It's important to consider the overall financial health of your company when deciding whether or not you should ask for a raise.

True. Your company may be in no position to grant raises because of a weak economy, poor management, or other factors. Timing is key when asking for a raise. If you ask for a raise during bad economic times, your boss may think you are oblivious to the company's problems or simply self-centered.

IN SUMMARY . . .

- Evaluate your work performance and employment period before approaching your boss for a raise.

- Ask for, never demand, a raise.

- When hoping for a raise, be realistic about the amount of pay increase you expect to receive. Have your boss suggest an amount first.

- Consider the financial health of your company before asking for a raise. If business has been slow, wait until things pick up again.

14

WHEN TO MOVE ON

Sooner or later, the day will come when it's time to leave your job. Perhaps you see the business going down the tubes. Perhaps you've found a better job. Perhaps you've decided this isn't the occupation for you. Or maybe you just dislike this particular workplace and want to move to another. Whatever your reasons, there are certain things you have to do to prepare yourself for moving on.

DECIDING TO LEAVE

First, ask yourself several questions: Is it in my best interest to move on? Will my life improve, income increase, or goals come one step closer if I accept a different opportunity? Do I really want to leave this job, or am I just bored? Will I be happier in a different working environment? Am I cut out for this industry?

Then you should ask yourself practical questions: Do I have another job to move into, or am I going to have to survive on savings until the next one comes

✔ TRUE OR FALSE?

Will You Know When It's Time to Get a New Job?

1. Giving one-week's notice is enough if I decide to leave my job.

2. Letters of recommendation are useful tools during the job search.

3. It's okay to badmouth your employer or company once you give your notice.

Test yourself as you read through this chapter. The answers appear on pages 142–143.

along? Can I do without the salary or benefits I have with this job? What will I do about health and dental coverage, life insurance, and a retirement plan?

The answers to these and other questions that will inevitably come to mind will be ruled by your instincts. You'll know when it's time to move on.

For many people a job is more than an income—it's an important part of who we are. So a career transition of any sort is one of the most unsettling experiences you can face in your life.

—Paul Clitheroe, Australian television presenter and financial analyst

LEAVING FOR THE RIGHT REASONS

The following two scenarios are examples of people who make well-informed choices about leaving their jobs:

- Trisha loved her job as a receptionist at a modeling agency. She loved the work, she loved the people, and she loved the challenges of her demanding and glamorous job. After a while, however, she decided that she wasn't following her dreams. After looking at headshot after headshot, she realized that she wanted to see her own face in the picture. She didn't want to be a receptionist for a modeling agency; she wanted to be a model. Answering phones and booking appointments wasn't in her heart. So she gave her two-week notice and embarked on her new career.

- Devon was bored in his job. He'd been in the same position for two years, hoping that a supervisor position was going to open up soon. It didn't. Devon started to wonder if he was in a dead-end job, one that wasn't going to allow him much opportunity to move up the ranks of the chain of command. He was stuck in a low-level job at low-level pay. If he wanted to afford college tuition, he knew he had to find a better position—one with more opportunities—and decided to move on.

In order to leave your job, you must give your boss advance warning that you'll be leaving your position. This is often called giving your *two-week notice,* because you should give your boss no less than two weeks to find someone to replace you. Many people suggest you give a week's notice for each year you've worked for the company, up to six weeks. If you have already landed a new job, your new employer may want you to start as soon as possible, but most employers should respect you for wanting to give your current employer a final two weeks. After all, wouldn't this new employer want you to give them the same consideration?

Go directly to your supervisor and let him or her know that you're giving your notice. Your supervisor will ask you to submit your official notice either in writing or in person to the manager or the head boss.

"The boss was sorry to see me go," says Kayla. "In fact, she tried to get me to stay. She even offered me a raise. That was hard to pass up, but I already had a better job waiting for me."

If you're leaving on good terms, ask your boss for a *letter of recommendation.* In this type of letter, your boss will write something similar to the following example.

The letter of recommendation you receive from your boss is a useful tool in the search for your next job. As a matter of fact, some employers require letters of recommendation from prospective employees.

SAMPLE LETTER OF RECOMMENDATION

Crawden Associates, Inc.
1111 Main Street
Anytown, NY 10010

To whom it may concern:

For 18 months, Matt Smith demonstrated
excellent skills and professionalism in his
capacity as our communications director.
He has always been dependable, trustworthy,
and a credit to our company.

Matt proved that he is capable under
pressure, organized, and a real team player.
His last several evaluation reports have been
outstanding, and we are happy to give our
full recommendations to this outstanding
employee.

Sincerely,

Samantha Jones

LEAVE ON GOOD TERMS

No matter how unhappy you've been at a job, once
you give notice try to leave on the best terms possible. Don't badmouth the company, your boss, or
your coworkers. Also, don't think you can use your

last two weeks to slack off and coast along until your last day.

Bosses have ways of getting back at you, so always be sure that you stay on good terms with former employers. You don't want to cringe, three or four years from now, when someone at a company you're desperate to work for says, "I'd really like you to join our team. I'll call you as soon as I've spoken with some of your former supervisors." As the saying goes, "Don't burn your bridges."

THE SCOOP ON EXIT INTERVIEWS

If you have voluntarily resigned your position, your employer may ask you to participate in an exit interview. During an exit interview, you meet with at least one individual from your company's human resources department, who will ask you questions that are formulated to help the company retain employees and improve working conditions. (Note: Some companies conduct exit interviews by asking departing employees to complete an electronic questionnaire, rather than participate in a face-to-face interview.)

Although many companies conduct exit interviews for legitimate reasons, other companies have ulterior motives when conducting the interviews, according to About.com. They use the information from the interviews to protect themselves against possible litigation if an employee decides to sue them for discrimination or harassment at a later date.

Should you participate in an exit interview? There is no consensus among career experts regarding exit interviews, and the choice is ultimately up to you. Consider the following pros and cons when deciding whether to participate in an exit interview:

Pros of Participating in an Exit Interview

- If you work for a reputable company, your feedback will help improve working conditions there.

Cons of Participating in an Exit Interview

- The information you provide may be used against you if you decide to sue your company for harassment, discrimination, etc.

- Information you provide could be used against you if the company is asked for references by a potential employer or is contacted for a background check.

About.com suggests that you ask yourself the following questions if asked to participate in an exit interview:

- How will I benefit from the interview?

- Will I be negatively impacted?

- Is the exit interview anonymous or do I have to give my name?

- What are my employer's goals for the interview—to improve the company or to protect itself against future litigation?

- Will not participating in the interview cause my employer to take retributive actions (providing negative references, etc.) against me?

- Was I harassed or discriminated against in any way during my tenure at the company? If so, is participating in the interview a good idea?

☞ FACT

Today's coworker may become tomorrow's supervisor, so maintain a professional attitude right through your last day.

Source: "Mistakes When Leaving a Job,"
http://www.allsands.com/Money/
jobemployment_oc_gn.htm

Finally, after deciding to leave a job, be sure to add to your resume the experiences and skills you learned from the job. Include any special projects you completed and any computer skills you learned.

✔ TRUE OR FALSE: ANSWERS

Will You Know When It's Time to Get a New Job?

1. Giving one-week's notice is enough if I decide to leave my job.

False. You should always give at least two-week's notice when you leave a job. It is the professional thing to do, and it encourages companies to speak positively of you when they are contacted for references. If you've been with a company for years and play a critical role in its daily operation, you should give a week's notice for each year you've worked at the company—up to six years.

2. Letters of recommendation are useful tools during the job search.

True. Competition for jobs is intense these days, and strong letters of recommendation will help you stick out from the crowd.

3. It's okay to badmouth your employer or company once you give your notice.

False. Talking poorly about your boss or employer is unprofessional, plus you don't want to burn bridges. In the future, you may need a reference from your manager, end up returning to the company, or work for one or more of your managers at a different company.

IN SUMMARY . . .

- Consider all the alternatives (and consequences) before you decide whether to move on to another job.

- Once you've decided to leave a job, give your supervisor no less than two weeks to prepare the department for your departure.

- Stay on good terms with your boss and coworkers; if possible, ask your immediate supervisor for a letter of recommendation.

- Revise your resume after leaving a job to include experiences and knowledge you gained from your former position.

WEB SITES

Body Language

Answers.com: Body Language
    http://www.answers.com/topic/body-language

Gestures: Body Language and Nonverbal
    Communication
    http://www.csupomona.edu/~tassi/gestures.
    htm#gestures

What the Boss' Body Language Says
    http://hotjobs.yahoo.com/career-articles-what_
    the_boss_body_language_says-306

Bosses

First30Days: How to Handle a New Boss
    http://www.first30days.com/starting-a-new-job/
    articles/how-to-handle-a-new-boss.html#

SeekingSuccess.com: Getting Along with Your Boss
    http://www.seekingsuccess.com/articles/art103.
    php

Yahoo! HotJobs: Getting on the Boss's Good Side
http://hotjobs.yahoo.com/career-articles-getting_on_the_boss_s_good_side-498

Communication Skills

MindTools: Communication Skills
http://www.mindtools.com/page8.html

Dress, Business

About.com: Business Casual Dress Code
http://humanresources.about.com/od/glossaryd/g/dress_code.htm

About.com: Getting Along with Your Boss and Co-Workers
http://careerplanning.about.com/od/bosscoworkers/Getting_Along_With_Your_Boss_and_CoWorkers.htm

About.com: How to Dress for Work and Interviews
http://careerplanning.about.com/cs/dressingforwork/a/dress_success.htm

AskMen.com: Business Casual Outfits
http://www.askmen.com/fashion/trends/21_fashion_men.html

Business Casual Attire
http://www.career.vt.edu/JOBSEARC/BusCasual.htm

How to Dress Business Casual—Men
http://www.ehow.com/how_41_dress-business-casual.html

How to Dress Business Casual—Women
http://www.ehow.com/how_49_dress-business-casual.html

wikiHow: How to Dress For Work
http://www.wikihow.com/Dress-for-Work

Yahoo! HotJobs: The Rules of Workplace Style
http://hotjobs.yahoo.com/career-articles-the_rules_of_workplace_style-535

General

About.com: Workplace Survival and Success
http://careerplanning.about.com/od/workplace-survival/Workplace_Survival_and_Success.htm

First Day on the Job
http://www.laworks.net/Youth_Portal/YP_Forms/YP_FirstDay.pdf

GradView
http://www.gradview.com/careers/etiquette.html

How Stuff Works: How Fax Machines Work
http://communication.howstuffworks.com/fax-machine4.htm

How to Use a Scanner
http://www.aarp.org/learntech/computers/howto/Articles/a2002-07-16-scan.html

Manners International
http://www.mannersinternational.com

MindTools: Essential Skills for an Excellent Career
http://www.mindtools.com

Work911.com
http://www.work911.com

Harassment

Equality and Human Rights Commission
http://www.equalityhumanrights.com

Equal Employment Opportunity Commission
http://www.eeoc.gov

Harassment Hotline Inc.
http://www.end-harassment.com

Women's Rights at Work
http://www.citizenactionny.org

WorkRelationships Inc.
http://www.workrelationships.com

Job Search

CollegeGrad.com: Resumes
http://www.collegegrad.com/resume

The Riley Guide: Resumes & Cover Letters
http://www.rileyguide.com/letters.html

Vault.com: Resumes and Advice
http://www.vault.com/index.jsp

Yahoo! HotJobs: Interviewing
http://hotjobs.yahoo.com/interview

Labor Laws

elaws: Fair Labor Standards Act Advisor

http://www.dol.gov/elaws/flsa.htm

Equal Employment Opportunity Commission
http://www.eeoc.gov

U.S. Department of Labor: Employment Standards
Administration
http://www.dol.gov/esa/whd/flsa

Youth Rules!
http://www.youthrules.dol.gov

Money Management

eHow: How to Save Money
http://www.ehow.com/how_2256041_save-money.html

Debt-Proof Living
http://www.cheapskatemonthly.com

The Motley Fool
http://www.fool.com

SavingAdvice.com
http://www.savingadvice.com

SavingSecrets
http://www.savingsecrets.com

66 Ways to Save Money
http://www.pueblo.gsa.gov/cic_text/
money/66ways/content

YoungInvestor.com
http://www.younginvestor.com

Office Politics

About.com: Office Politics
http://careerplanning.about.com/od/
workplacesurvival/a/politics.htm

About.com: Workplace Survival and Success
http://careerplanning.about.com/od/workplace-
survival/Workplace_Survival_and_Success.htm

Ask Sue: Workplace Cliques
http://www.careerknowhow.com/ask_sue/clique.
htm

Monster.com: Winning at Office Politics: Master
the Game By Making Connections
http://career-advice.monster.com/office-politics/
diversity-inclusion/multicultural-workers/
Winning-at-Office-Politics/home.aspx

Office-Politics
http://www.officepolitics.com

Office Skills

Expert Village: Learn Basic Computer Skills
http://www.expertvillage.com/video-series/528_
computer-filing-system-windows.htm

How Stuff Works: How Fax Machines Work
http://communication.howstuffworks.com/fax-
machine4.htm

How Stuff Works: How Virtual Offices Work
http://communication.howstuffworks.com/
virtual-office.htm

How to Use a Scanner
   http://www.aarp.org/learntech/computers/
   howto/Articles/a2002-07-16-scan.html

Salary

About.com: How to Ask for a Raise
   http://careerplanning.about.com/od/
   negotiatingoffers/a/raise.htm

Forbes.com: Seven No-Nos When Asking for a
   Raise
   http://www.forbes.com/2006/01/04/careers-
   work-employment-cx_sr_0105bizbasics_print.
   html

Glassdoor.com
   http://www.glassdoor.com

JobStar Central
   http://jobstar.org

Nonprofit Salaries
   http://www.idealist.org/en/career/salarysurvey.
   html

PayScale.com: How to Make Money in a Recession:
   Ask for a Raise
   http://www.payscale.com/ask-for-a-raise-during-
   recession

Salary.com
   http://www.salary.com

SalaryWebsite
   http://www.salarywebsite.com

U.S. Department of Labor: Salary Estimates
http://www.salarysurvey.org

Time Management

Time Management: You Versus the Clock
http://pbskids.org/itsmylife/school/time/index.
htm

GLOSSARY

benefits special services provided by an employer, such as health and dental coverage, retirement plans, and profit sharing

business mission the list of goals a company aims to achieve

casual Friday workday in which a company allows its employees to dress less formally than on other days of the week

chain of command the order of rank and power in a company

compensation time time off granted to a worker who has worked extra hours without pay

daily grind a slang term for a nine-to-five job

deductions amount taken out of a paycheck for taxes and other expenses

diplomacy skill in dealing with people through tact and mutual respect

discrimination treating a person with disfavor or prejudice, often based on race or gender

exit interview voluntary interview between an employee who is leaving a company and a member of the human resources department; can be used by a good company to retain employees and improve working conditions or by a disreputable company to gather information to protect itself against future legal action

feedback a reply or response to an idea, action, or proposal

for-profit organization an organization that operates with the intention of making a profit

401(k) plan a savings plan that sets aside money for retirement

harassment unlawful suggestive or abusive treatment directed toward a person

insurance coverage or protection against loss or illness

investment a financial contribution into an interest-earning account

letter of recommendation letter of reference from a former teacher, supervisor, or coworker that summarizes your work habits and personality traits; it's used to get into school or to land a job

net pay the amount of money taken home after taxes

nonexempt employees workers paid by the hour that are eligible for overtime compensation

nonprofit organization an organization that provides a service (often humanitarian in nature) and whose aim is not to make money but to earn enough to cover expenses and stay in operation

obligation a responsibility or duty

office politics dynamics of a workplace, often outside of a company's formal hierarchy and procedures, that can dictate the day-to-day proceedings in the office; often has negative connotation

overtime the period of time worked above and beyond regular job hours

personnel the employees of a company

policy a company's standard rules and regulations

profit the difference between total income and expenses

promotion advancement in pay or position within a company

punctuality being on time

references statements by employers and colleagues that attest to your qualities as an employee

resume a written list of your education and work experiences used to get a job or a promotion

revenue a company's total income before expenses

sexual harassment unlawful sexually suggestive or abusive treatment directed toward an individual by a manager or coworker or conditions of employment, hiring, promotions, and retention that are contingent on the victim providing sexual favors

superiors people of higher rank and position

termination the ending of a person's employment

time-and-a-half the rate of pay for overtime, equal to 1.5 times regular hourly wages

two-week notice the amount of notice (two weeks) that is customary to give an employer before leaving a job

BIBLIOGRAPHY

Ball, Michael. *You're Too Smart for This: Beating the 100 Big Lies About Your First Job.* Naperville, Ill.: Sourcebooks, 2006.

Baude, Dawn-Michelle. *The Executive Guide to E-mail Correspondence: Including Model Letters for Every Situation.* Franklin Lakes, N.J.: Career Press, 2006.

Boland, Mary. *Sexual Harassment in the Workplace.* Naperville, Ill.: Sphinx Publishing, 2005.

Coplin, William D. *10 Things Employers Want You to Learn in College: The Know-How You Need to Succeed.* Berkeley, Calif.: Ten Speed Press, 2003.

Covey, Sean. *The 7 Habits of Highly Effective Teens.* New York: Fireside Press, 1998.

Covey, Stephen R. *The 7 Habits of Highly Effective People.* 15th ed. New York: The Free Press, 2004.

Davidson, Jeff. *The Complete Idiot's Guide to Getting Things Done.* New York: Alpha, 2005.

————. *The Complete Idiot's Guide to Managing Your Time*. 3d ed. New York: Alpha, 2001.

Decker, Diane C., Victoria A. Hoevemeyer, and Marianne Rowe-Dimas. *First-Job Survival Guide: How To Thrive and Advance in Your New Career*. Indianapolis, Ind.: JIST Works, 2005.

Fox, Sue. *Etiquette For Dummies*. 2d ed. Hoboken, N.J.: For Dummies, 2007.

Freedman, Elizabeth. *Work 101: Learning the Ropes of the Workplace Without Hanging Yourself*. New York: Bantam Books, 2007.

Gregory, Raymond F. *Unwelcome and Unlawful: Sexual Harassment in the American Workplace*. Ithaca, N.Y.: Cornell University Press, 2004.

Hansen, Dhawn, and Tracey Turner. *Organize Your Office and Manage Your Time: A Be Smart Girls Guide*. Bloomington, Ind.: iUniverse Inc., 2007.

Harvard Business Essentials Guide to Negotiation. Cambridge, Mass.: Harvard Business School Press, 2003.

Henderson, Veronique, and Pat Henshaw. *Image Matters for Men: How to Dress for Success!* London, U.K.: Hamlyn, 2007.

Howard, Linda Gordon. *The Sexual Harassment Handbook*. Franklin Lakes, N.J.: Career Press, 2007.

Kaip, Sarah. *The Woman's Workplace Survival Guide*. Medford, Oreg.: Advantage Source, 2005.

Klaus, Peggy. *The Hard Truth About Soft Skills: Workplace Lessons Smart People Wish They'd Learned Sooner.* New York: Collins Business, 2008.

Lenius, Oscar. *A Well-Dressed Gentleman's Pocket Guide.* London, U.K.: Prion, 2006.

Lerner, Dick. *Dress Like the Big Fish: How to Achieve the Image You Want and the Success You Deserve.* Omaha, Neb.: Bel Air Fashions Press, 2008.

Levy, Anne C., and Michele A. Paludi. *Workplace Sexual Harassment.* 2d ed. Upper Saddle River, N.J.: Prentice Hall, 2001.

Malhotra, Deepak, and Max Bazerman. *Negotiation Genius: How to Overcome Obstacles and Achieve Brilliant Results at the Bargaining Table and Beyond.* New York: Bantam, 2008.

Miller, Patrick W. *Body Language on the Job.* Munster, Ind.: Patrick W. Miller & Associates, 2006.

Peres, Daniel. *Details Men's Style Manual: The Ultimate Guide for Making Your Clothes Work for You.* New York: Gotham, 2007.

Reiman, Tonya. *The Power of Body Language.* New York: Pocket, 2007.

Seligson, Hannah. *New Girl on the Job: Advice from the Trenches.* New York: Citadel, 2007.

Shea, Gregory, and Robert E. Gunther. *Your Job Survival Guide: A Manual for Thriving in Change.* Upper Saddle River, N.J.: FT Press, 2008.

Shell, G. Richard. *Bargaining for Advantage: Negotiation Strategies for Reasonable People.* 2d ed. New York: Penguin Books, 2006.

Sindell, Milo, and Thuy Sindell. *Sink or Swim!: New Job. New Boss. 12 Weeks to Get It Right.* 2d ed. Cincinnati, Ohio: Adams Media, 2006.

Tieger, Paul D., and Barbara Barron. *Do What You Are: Discover the Perfect Career for You Through the Secrets of Personality Type.* Rev. ed. New York: Little, Brown and Company, 2007.

Weingarten, Rachel C. *Career and Corporate Cool.* Hoboken, N.J.: Wiley, 2007.

Index